D. Hurlburt   S0-BOK-624

60 Must-Have

GRAPHIC ORGANIZERS

by Ginger Baggette

Carson-Dellosa Publishing LLC
Greensboro, North Carolina

Credits

Content Editor: Christine Schwab
Copy Editor: Julie B. Killian
Layout and Cover Design: Lori Jackson
Inside Illustrations: Julie Kinlaw

Carson-Dellosa Publishing LLC
PO Box 35665
Greensboro, NC 27425 USA
www.carsondellosa.com

© 2012, Carson-Dellosa Publishing LLC. The purchase of this material entitles the buyer to reproduce worksheets and activities for classroom use only—not for commercial resale. Reproduction of these materials for an entire school or district is prohibited. No part of this book may be reproduced (except as noted above), stored in a retrieval system, or transmitted in any form or by any means (mechanically, electronically, recording, etc.) without the prior written consent of Carson-Dellosa Publishing LLC.

Printed in the USA • All rights reserved.

ISBN 978-1-60996-473-3
02-205121151

Table of Contents

Graphic Organizer Title	Pages	Predicting	Math	Science	Social Studies	Recalling/Locating	Predicting	Comparing/Contrasting	Summarizing	Classifying/Categorizing	Ordering/Prioritizing	Organizing/Planning	Explaining	Analyzing	Identifying	Sorting	Drawing Conclusions	Justifying	Problem Solving	Evaluating/Reflecting	Investigating	Sequencing
		Subject Areas				**Remember**	**Understand**					**Apply**		**Analyze**				**Evaluate**			**Create**	
A Picture-Perfect Story Frame	8	✓			✓	✓			✓	✓		✓	✓	✓	✓	✓	✓					
A Whale of a Tale	10	✓		✓	✓	✓			✓	✓		✓	✓	✓	✓	✓	✓					
Considering a Character	12	✓			✓	✓			✓	✓		✓	✓	✓	✓	✓	✓			✓		
Popcorn Predictions	14	✓	✓	✓	✓		✓					✓	✓	✓			✓		✓	✓	✓	
Blooming Details	16	✓			✓				✓	✓	✓		✓	✓	✓	✓	✓	✓		✓		
Constructing Conclusions	18	✓	✓	✓	✓	✓	✓		✓	✓		✓	✓	✓	✓	✓	✓		✓	✓		✓
Taking a Bite Out of a Circle Map	20	✓	✓	✓	✓	✓			✓	✓		✓		✓	✓	✓				✓		
Shining a Light on Bright Ideas	22	✓	✓	✓	✓	✓		✓	✓	✓		✓	✓	✓	✓						✓	✓
Composing Connections	24	✓	✓	✓	✓	✓	✓	✓				✓	✓	✓	✓		✓	✓		✓		
A Picture Is Worth a Thousand Words	26	✓	✓	✓	✓	✓			✓	✓	✓	✓	✓	✓	✓		✓		✓	✓	✓	✓
Inspecting for Evidence	28	✓	✓	✓	✓	✓	✓		✓			✓	✓	✓	✓		✓	✓	✓	✓	✓	
Coat of Arms	30	✓		✓	✓	✓			✓	✓		✓	✓	✓	✓	✓				✓		
Pieces of a Puzzle	32	✓			✓	✓			✓	✓	✓	✓	✓	✓				✓	✓	✓		✓
Spinning Summaries	34	✓	✓	✓	✓	✓	✓		✓	✓		✓	✓	✓	✓		✓			✓	✓	✓
Writing Around the World	36	✓	✓	✓	✓	✓	✓	✓	✓	✓	✓	✓	✓	✓	✓	✓	✓	✓	✓	✓	✓	✓
Don't Judge a Book by Its Cover	38	✓			✓	✓		✓	✓	✓		✓	✓	✓	✓		✓	✓		✓		
The Daily Times	40	✓			✓	✓		✓	✓	✓	✓	✓	✓	✓			✓	✓		✓		✓
Wordy Wagons	42	✓			✓	✓		✓	✓					✓	✓							✓
Tickets Back in Time	44	✓		✓	✓	✓			✓	✓	✓	✓	✓	✓	✓		✓				✓	✓
Fast-Track Flowchart	46	✓	✓	✓	✓	✓			✓	✓		✓	✓	✓								✓
Get Your Ducks in a Row	48	✓	✓	✓	✓	✓			✓	✓		✓	✓	✓	✓							✓
Stepping Through a Storyboard	50	✓			✓	✓			✓	✓	✓	✓	✓	✓			✓					✓
Circling Through a Cycle	52	✓		✓	✓	✓			✓	✓	✓	✓	✓	✓			✓		✓	✓		✓
Riding a Chain of Events	54	✓		✓	✓	✓			✓	✓	✓	✓		✓	✓							✓
Royal Rankings	56	✓	✓	✓					✓	✓	✓		✓	✓	✓	✓	✓		✓	✓		✓
What Is My Question? Find the Answer	58	✓	✓	✓	✓	✓	✓					✓	✓	✓			✓		✓		✓	
Corralling a Cluster Map	60	✓	✓	✓	✓	✓		✓		✓		✓	✓	✓	✓	✓	✓		✓	✓		
Climbing Through a Tree Map	62	✓	✓	✓	✓	✓		✓		✓		✓		✓					✓	✓		
Spinning a Web	64	✓	✓	✓	✓			✓	✓	✓		✓	✓	✓	✓	✓	✓				✓	
A Penny for Your Thoughts	66	✓	✓	✓	✓	✓	✓	✓	✓	✓		✓	✓	✓	✓		✓	✓	✓	✓	✓	✓

CD-104533 © Carson-Dellosa

Skills Matrix

Graphic Organizer Title	Pages	Subject Areas — Predicting	Math	Science	Social Studies	Remember — Recalling/Locating	Predicting	Understand — Comparing/Contrasting	Summarizing	Classifying/Categorizing	Apply — Ordering/Prioritizing	Organizing/Planning	Explaining	Analyze — Analyzing	Identifying	Sorting	Drawing Conclusions	Evaluate — Justifying	Problem Solving	Evaluating/Reflecting	Create — Investigating	Sequencing
Navigating Through Notes	68	✓	✓	✓	✓	✓	✓		✓			✓	✓	✓	✓		✓	✓			✓	✓
Ready, Set, Research	70	✓		✓	✓	✓		✓	✓	✓	✓	✓	✓	✓	✓	✓	✓	✓	✓	✓	✓	✓
Stirring Up Success	72		✓	✓	✓		✓			✓	✓	✓	✓	✓	✓		✓		✓	✓	✓	
Engaging Experiments	74			✓			✓				✓	✓	✓				✓	✓	✓	✓	✓	
A Spotted Survey	76		✓	✓		✓		✓		✓		✓	✓	✓	✓	✓	✓				✓	✓
Diving into Data	78		✓	✓		✓		✓	✓			✓	✓	✓	✓	✓	✓				✓	✓
Sticky-Sweet Sorting	80		✓	✓		✓									✓							
A Sporty Sort	82		✓	✓		✓									✓							
Just Me as a T	84		✓	✓	✓						✓				✓							
One Sharp KWL	86	✓	✓	✓	✓	✓	✓	✓				✓	✓	✓	✓		✓	✓			✓	✓
One Rule for the Bunch	88	✓	✓	✓		✓		✓	✓	✓	✓	✓	✓	✓	✓	✓		✓			✓	
It's All in the Bag	90	✓	✓	✓		✓		✓	✓			✓	✓	✓	✓	✓		✓	✓			✓
Sign It with a Y	92	✓		✓	✓	✓		✓	✓			✓	✓	✓	✓			✓	✓	✓		
Weighing In on Fact and Opinion	94	✓		✓	✓	✓		✓	✓	✓			✓	✓	✓		✓	✓	✓	✓		
Pros or Cons	96	✓									✓	✓	✓	✓	✓	✓	✓	✓	✓	✓	✓	✓
Raining Cause and Effect	98	✓		✓	✓	✓		✓	✓			✓	✓	✓	✓	✓	✓	✓	✓	✓	✓	✓
Something Is a Little Fishy	100	✓		✓	✓	✓		✓	✓				✓		✓			✓			✓	
A Colorful Matrix	102	✓	✓	✓	✓	✓	✓	✓	✓	✓	✓	✓	✓	✓	✓		✓				✓	✓
A Magnificent Map	104		✓		✓	✓			✓	✓		✓	✓	✓	✓					✓	✓	
I Spy a PMI Chart	106	✓	✓	✓	✓	✓	✓	✓	✓	✓		✓	✓	✓	✓		✓	✓	✓	✓	✓	
A Window into Words	108	✓	✓	✓	✓	✓		✓	✓			✓		✓	✓							
Pedaling Through a Problem	110		✓	✓			✓		✓			✓	✓	✓			✓	✓	✓	✓		✓
Exit This Way	112	✓	✓	✓	✓	✓		✓	✓	✓		✓	✓	✓			✓	✓	✓	✓		
All Boxed In	114	✓	✓	✓	✓	✓		✓	✓	✓		✓	✓	✓			✓		✓	✓		
Taking Time to Reflect	116	✓	✓	✓	✓	✓			✓			✓	✓	✓	✓				✓	✓		
Inching Our Way to Success	118	✓	✓	✓	✓	✓	✓	✓	✓		✓	✓	✓	✓			✓	✓	✓			
Actions Speak Louder Than Words	120	✓	✓	✓	✓	✓	✓	✓	✓			✓	✓	✓			✓	✓	✓			
Assignment Banners	122	✓	✓	✓	✓	✓	✓	✓	✓	✓	✓	✓	✓				✓	✓	✓			
Reading Log	124	✓	✓	✓	✓	✓			✓			✓		✓	✓		✓		✓			
A Packed Portfolio	126	✓	✓	✓	✓	✓			✓	✓	✓		✓			✓			✓			

Introduction

As the demands of the classroom increase, one way to support teachers and students is through the use of graphic organizers. Graphic organizers are visual templates designed to help students understand relationships between facts and ideas. Using graphic organizers is a quick and easy way to deliver instruction, allowing each student to structure ideas in a way that enhances recall, problem solving, and decision making. Graphic organizers are also ideal for students to practice higher-order thinking skills while they analyze information and create written pieces. We are delighted that you have chosen *60 Must-Have Graphic Organizers* and are sure that you will discover a multitude of uses and benefits as you turn each page.

Who should use these organizers?

As classroom dynamics change from year to year, so do the needs of students. For this reason, teachers must have differentiating and accessible tools that meet the needs of a diverse group of learners. *60 Must-Have Graphic Organizers* was developed with a range of ages, ability levels, and learning styles in mind. The graphic organizers are ideal for any classroom and beneficial for all students and teachers.

What are some ways that you can use these organizers in your classroom?

Each category in this book contains graphic organizers that touch on a variety of skills. The organizers are perfect for use in whole-group, small-group, or individual settings. They can be tiered for use with ability groups, enlarged and placed on the board for whole-group instruction, or used as tools for group or peer work. The organizers are ideal to use for the following:

- Pre-assessments
- Organizational tools
- Study guides
- Assessments
- Research templates
- Data collection
- Brainstorming models
- Reflection pieces
- Prewriting tools
- And much more!

When should you use graphic organizers?

Graphic organizers are designed for use during all phases of learning (before, during, and after instruction). The collection of organizers in *60 Must-Have Graphic Organizers* is filled with material that will activate prior knowledge and organize learning during instruction. The organizers are ideal for both formative and summative assessment and perfect for workstations or learning centers.

CD-104533 ■ © Carson-Dellosa

Introduction

Where do the organizers fit during classroom instruction?

Graphic organizers have had their place in reading instruction for many years. However, they are fast becoming everyday tools that are beneficial in other curricular areas. Because the organizers in this collection are multifunctional, many can be used across the curriculum and are ideal in standard and special education classroom settings. While all of the organizers fit into at least two or more subject areas, most all of them can be used in the following subject areas:

- Language Arts
- Math
- Science
- Social Studies
- Character Education

Many of the organizers are also useful for student planning and organization. The possibilities are endless!

Why is it important to use graphic organizers when teaching?

The use of graphic organizers can impact performance and overall learning. With high-stakes standardized testing, it is important that classrooms today be equipped with material that will help students make connections to their learning, organize their ideas, and use higher-order thinking skills. This is what makes *60 Must-Have Graphic Organizers* so unique. The collection is designed to provide students with a visual structure for organization but also takes learning to the next level by asking students to reflect on and analyze their thinking. Each organizer encourages students to solve problems and think creatively.

How do you get started with this collection of organizers?

Getting started is simple. The organizers contained in this book are set up in an easy-to-use format. The names of the organizers are listed in the table of contents by categories, and a skills matrix identifies the subject areas and skills covered by each organizer. Within the book, each organizer also includes subject areas and skills covered, as well as an explained purpose and a how-to section that will help with ideas and suggest ways to use the organizer.

The only limitation for the organizers included in this collection is your own imagination! What are you waiting for? Let's get started!

A Picture-Perfect Story Frame

Subject Area Uses
- Language Arts
- Social Studies

Skills
- Identifying story elements
- Understanding why story elements are critical
- Brainstorming as a way of prewriting and organizing details
- Classifying information

Purpose

All stories have something in common—story elements. Understanding story elements, such as characters, settings, problems, events, and solutions, is important for reading comprehension and story writing. Useful with a variety of texts, A Picture-Perfect Story Frame enhances understanding and promotes recall. The organizer is an essential tool for differentiating instruction with leveled readers or to use in a writing center.

Using This Graphic Organizer

A Picture-Perfect Story Frame creates a visually organized way for students to identify story elements from a text or from their own writing. Model the use of A Picture-Perfect Story Frame by placing a large copy on the board. Ask students to use it to describe a story recently read by the class as a group.

The organizer is useful in many other ways:

- Reading: identifying a story's title, author, illustrator, and story events in a whole-group, small-group, or literacy workstation
- Writing: brainstorming original stories
- Social Studies: helping struggling students break apart specific information, such as from a mini-lesson on American Indians, so that they see how each part is critical to the story as a whole.

Primary Model

This kindergarten student used the organizer to record the story elements in *The Royal Broomstick* by Heather Amery (Usborne Books, 2003). By using the organizer, the student began to see how the setting played an important role in the development of the story.

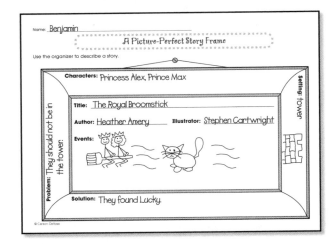

Intermediate Model

This fifth-grade student used the organizer in a social studies class to identify story elements from the historical fiction text *Number the Stars* by Lois Lowry (Laurel Leaf, 1989). Through the use of the diagram, the student was able to draw parallels between what he read and what he learned about that time in history.

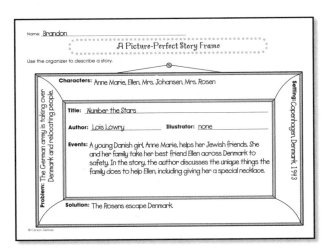

CD-104533 © Carson-Dellosa

Name: _____

A Picture-Perfect Story Frame

Use the organizer to describe a story.

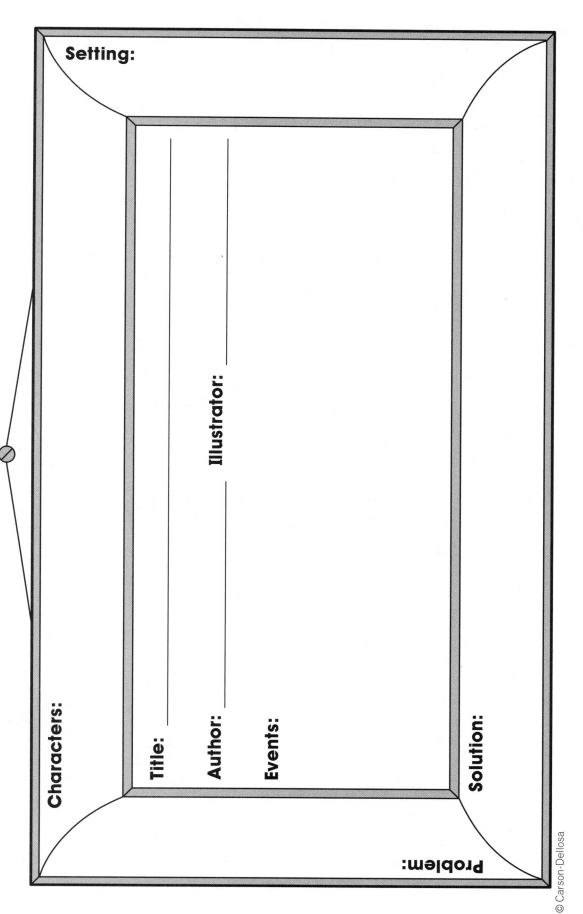

Setting:

Characters:

Title: _____

Author: _____

Illustrator: _____

Events:

Problem:

Solution:

© Carson-Dellosa

A Whale of a Tale

Subject Area Uses
- Language Arts
- Literary texts used in Science, Math, and Social Studies

Skills
- Recalling and summarizing information
- Analyzing text
- Brainstorming for writing

Purpose
Brainstorming and recalling information are vital skills for improving comprehension. A Whale of a Tale is an organizer that enables students to summarize their learning with clearly directed questions. The questions lead to brainstorming situations that allow students to think critically and create ideas for writing. The visual structure of the organizer engages students and helps them prioritize details. The organizer is useful in a variety of subject areas and with students of varied ability levels and learning styles.

Using This Graphic Organizer
Model the use of A Whale of a Tale by placing a large copy on the board. Ask students to identify *who, what, when, where, why,* and *how* from a story read aloud or from a new piece of writing.

The organizer is useful in many other ways:

- Reading: recalling, organizing, and summarizing information read from a variety of texts
- Writing: brainstorming an original story (written by an individual student or a small group) that is later developed into a completed written piece in a writing workstation
- Character Education: processing a peer situation in which students disagree, such as which group of students can use a piece of playground equipment, and later, role-playing an appropriate choice

Primary Model
This first-grade student used A Whale of a Tale for a writing assignment about an imaginary whale named Wally. The organizer allowed the student to place his ideas in a format that would help him begin his rough draft.

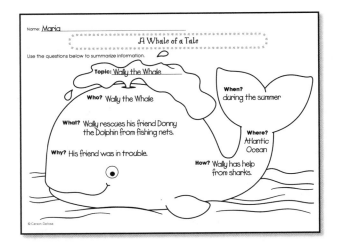

Intermediate Model
This fourth-grade student used A Whale of a Tale to complete a biographical study on Elizabeth Lucas Pinckney. By organizing the information, the student was able to retell what was learned about the historical figure. The organizer was also used as an assessment of learning to measure how much the student retained from the reading.

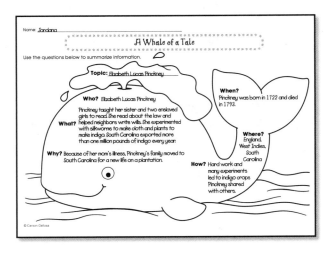

CD-104533 ■ © Carson-Dellosa

Name: _____

A Whale of a Tale

Use the questions below to summarize information.

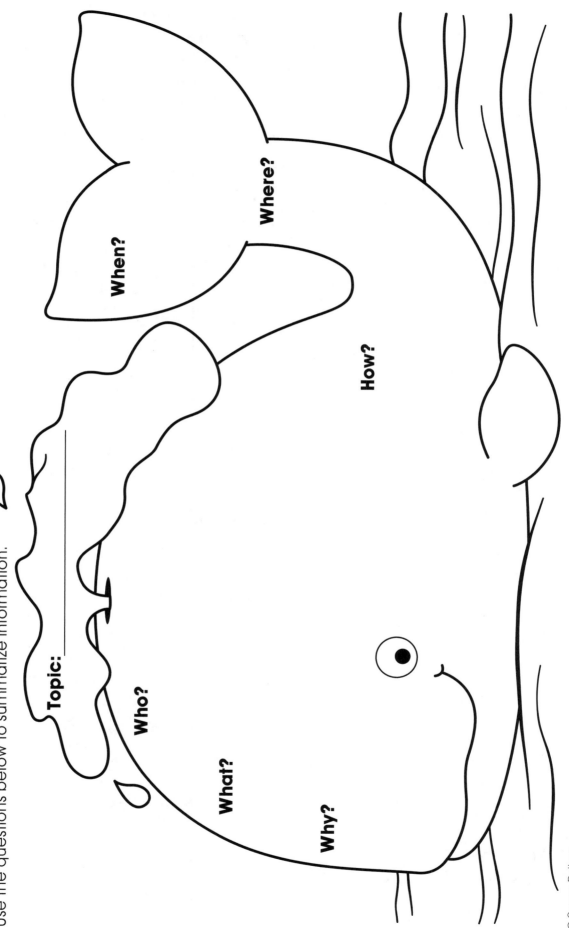

Topic: _____

When?

Where?

How?

Who?

What?

Why?

© Carson-Dellosa

Subject Area Uses

- Language Arts
- Literary texts used in Social Studies, Science, and Math

Skills

- Identifying character traits
- Using context clues to infer information about characters
- Creating traits of characters through writing

Purpose

Analyzing details about a character is important to comprehension of text. Considering a Character is an organizer designed to help students identify key characteristics about a character to support their understanding of the character and the story as a whole. Understanding the fine details is essential to helping students develop meaning and make characters come alive. This is crucial for students who struggle to make connections with characters they read or write about. The organizer is ideal to use with students of varied ability levels and in different subject areas.

Using This Graphic Organizer

Model the use of Considering a Character by placing a large copy on the board. Ask students to describe a character from a book read aloud. Then, have students answer the questions listed in each shape on the organizer.

The organizer is useful in many other ways:

- Reading: analyzing characters from a variety of texts during guided reading lessons or at a listening center
- Writing: brainstorming character traits about characters that students will use in their own original stories
- Social Studies: identifying details about a historical figure studied during a unit on famous women
- Science: identifying details during a group project in which students researched a famous scientist
- Math: using as an enrichment activity for a student who is interested in learning more about the Dewey Decimal System

Primary Model

This second-grade student used Considering a Character after reading *Beatrice Doesn't Want To* by Laura Numeroff (Candlewick, 2008) at a listening center during reading class. By using the organizer and looking critically at the characteristics and actions of the character described, the student learned that while Beatrice was very stubborn and always said no, she was really nice after all. The student also determined that Beatrice would have had more fun if she had not been so cranky.

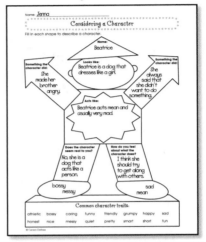

Intermediate Model

This third-grade teacher read *Ruby Bridges Goes to School: My True Story* by Ruby Bridges (Cartwheel Books, 2009) to her social studies class prior to teaching a lesson on segregation. This student used Considering a Character to list details from the story about Ruby and her life. By using the organizer, the student was able to create mental images of Ruby, which helped him better understand Ruby's story.

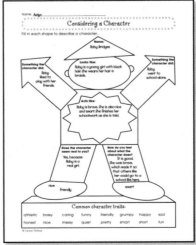

Name: _____

Fill in each shape to describe a character.

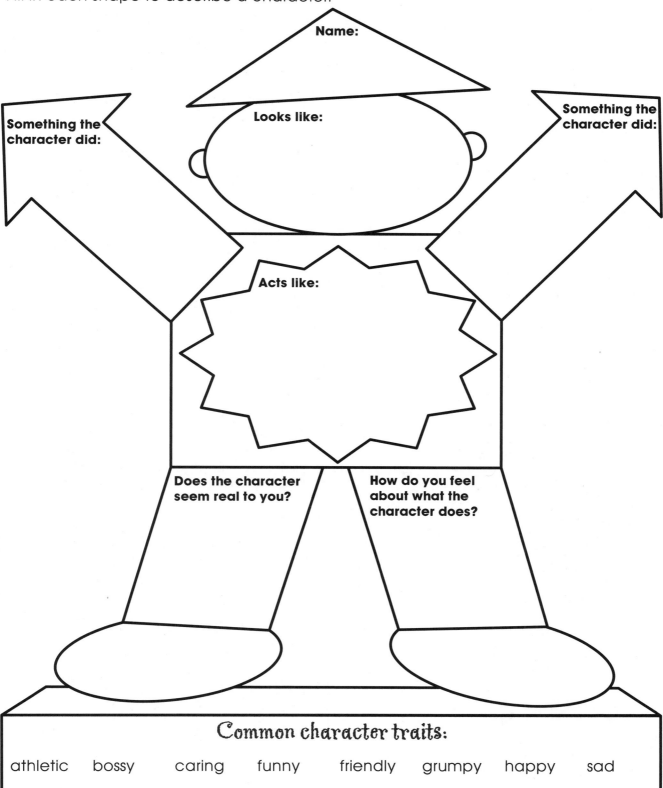

Name:

Looks like:

Something the character did:

Something the character did:

Acts like:

Does the character seem real to you?

How do you feel about what the character does?

Common character traits:

athletic	bossy	caring	funny	friendly	grumpy	happy	sad
honest	nice	messy	quiet	pretty	smart	short	fun

© Carson-Dellosa

Popcorn Predictions

Subject Area Uses
- Language arts
- Science
- Content-area literary texts used in Math, Social Studies, or Science

Objectives
- Making predictions
- Inferring information from context clues
- Reasoning

Purpose

A pre-reading strategy commonly used by teachers to promote comprehension is making predictions. Making good predictions is important to becoming a great reader. The Popcorn Predictions organizer is designed to help students with varied academic abilities increase their understanding and promote the use of higher-level thinking. With this organizer, students will stretch their imaginations and connect prior beliefs to new knowledge.

Using This Graphic Organizer

When students can connect new learning to prior knowledge, comprehension is better achieved. Teachers can model the use of Popcorn Predictions by having students take a picture walk through a text and use its context clues to predict what they think will happen. Here are some other ways for using the graphic organizer in the core subject areas:

- Reading: predicting what might happen in the first few chapters of the text after looking at the cover and the chapter titles
- Science: hypothesizing the outcome of a science experiment, such as mixing two or more ingredients or predicting the outcome of an informational text on a famous scientist
- Math: predicting what might happen if one of the factors or operations in a story problem changes
- Social Studies: drawing conclusions about what might happen next after reading a historical fiction text such as *Number the Stars* by Lois Lowry (Laurel Leaf, 1998)

Primary Model

This first-grade student used the Popcorn Predictions organizer in her small reading group while reading *All By Myself* by Mercer Mayer (Random House Books for Young Readers, 2001). The student was asked to take a picture walk through the book and make predictions about what she thought might happen before beginning to read. The organizer helped the student connect the pictures to what she already knew.

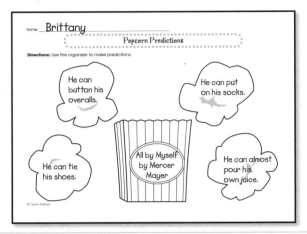

Intermediate Model

This fourth-grade student used the Popcorn Predictions in science class where he conducted an experiment on the outcome of mixing water and cornstarch. Using the organizer allowed the student to use his senses to predict what would happen using his senses.

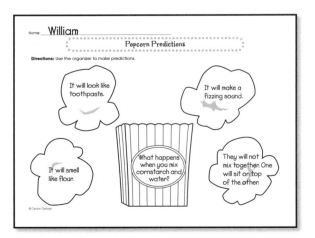

CD-104533 ■ © Carson-Dellosa

Name: _____

Popcorn Predictions

Use the organizer to make predictions.

© Carson-Dellosa

Blooming Details

Subject Area Uses
- Language Arts
- Social Studies

Skills
- Determining main idea and details
- Recalling information
- Making text-to-self connections
- Prewriting
- Organizing and summarizing information

Purpose

To fully comprehend what is read, students must develop the ability to analyze main ideas and details and their relationships to a story. The Blooming Details organizer is ideal for visually organizing information so that students see such relationships. This engaging organizer is perfect for differentiating learning because students of all ability levels can use it, depending on the amount and sophistication of each listed detail. The structure also provides space for students to reflect on what they have learned.

Using This Graphic Organizer

Blooming Details allows students to gain a better understanding of what substantiates the main idea of a story. Model the use of the organizer by having students write the main idea in the center circle and related details in the petals. Then, have students extend their learning by making connections to their work in the flowerpots.

The organizer is useful in many other ways:

- Reading: determining main ideas and details from literary texts used in guided reading or working with a student who is having difficulty understanding a story
- Writing: serving as a prewriting tool that can be used later during a student conference where feedback will be given before the student begins a rough draft
- Social Studies: summarizing learning about a historical figure and his or her accomplishments

Primary Model

This kindergarten student used Blooming Details in a reading center with the kindergarten assistant while reading a sight-word book entitled *Helpers* by Linda Ward Beech (Scholastic, 2003). The student listed the main idea in the center of the flower and then described helpful jobs in each petal. By using the organizer, the student learned how to organize and summarize information read, as well as thought about what kind of helper she might want to be when she grows up.

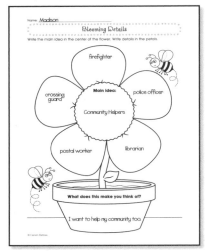

Intermediate Model

This fourth-grade student used Blooming Details in writing class to write a story about how his pet puppy grew into a dog. By using the organizer as a prewriting tool, the student was able to organize his ideas before writing his final draft. It also enabled him to connect what he was writing to his own thoughts about growing up.

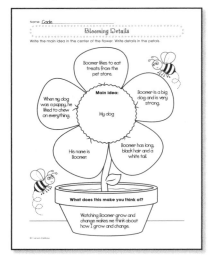

Name:_____

Blooming Details

Write the main idea in the center of the flower. Write details in the petals.

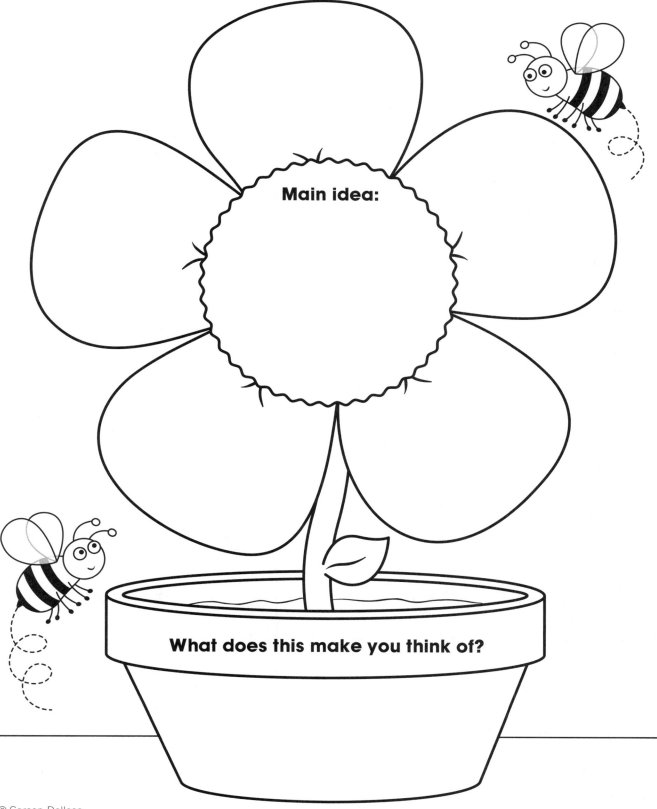

Main idea:

What does this make you think of?

© Carson-Dellosa

Constructing Conclusions

Subject Area Uses
- Language Arts
- Science

Skills
- Drawing conclusions
- Making inferences and predicting outcomes
- Identifying and analyzing information

Purpose

One of the most important skills needed to promote comprehension is the ability to make an inference or draw a conclusion. When students draw conclusions about a story, they are required to think critically and analyze information learned. Constructing Conclusions is designed with this kind of thinking in mind. The organizer is a tool that requires students to use higher-order thinking skills as they carefully analyze details related to a topic or something read.

Using This Graphic Organizer

Fact finding and reasoning are important to a student's ability to predict outcomes and develop the ability to analyze information. As children draw conclusions independently, they gain a broader understanding of topics. Constructing conclusions can be used in a variety of ways:

- Reading: making inferences about the outcome of a story or its characters based on details read or pictured during a guided reading lesson
- Writing: serving as a prewriting tool for a pair of students where one writes three pieces of evidence for which the other must provide a conclusion (can be used later during a class discussion)
- Science: drawing conclusions about an animal's food source or about how matter is altered when the temperature is changed

Primary Model

This second-grade student used Constructing Conclusions during a language arts lesson after reading several books about lions. The organizer allowed the student to record information she learned from the text, creating a visual record that enabled her to draw conclusions about the animal's abilities.

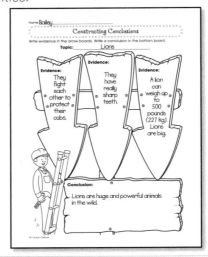

Intermediate Model

This fourth-grade student used Constructing Conclusions during science class while experimenting with heat, energy, and matter. In the experiment, the student heated several beverages and recorded what he saw. From there, the organizer helped him draw conclusions about what happens when matter is affected by heat.

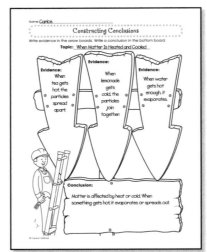

 CD-104533 ▩ © Carson-Dellosa

Name: _____

Constructing Conclusions

Write evidence in the arrow boards. Write a conclusion in the bottom board.

Topic: _____

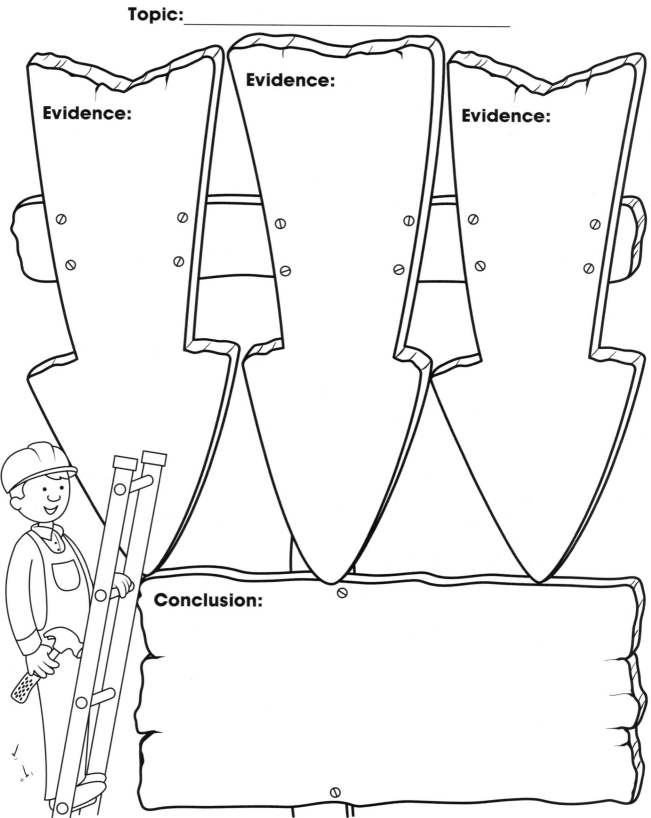

Evidence:

Evidence:

Evidence:

Conclusion:

© Carson-Dellosa

Taking a Bite Out of a Circle Map

Subject Area Uses
- Language Arts
- Social Studies
- Science
- Math
- Character Education

Skills
- Brainstorming
- Prewriting
- Recalling prior knowledge
- Making connections

Purpose

Activating prior knowledge is critical to new learning. Taking a Bite Out of a Circle Map is designed to visually engage students and help them showcase prior learning or brainstorm new ideas. The simple design of the organizer gives students the freedom to be creative and think critically about a topic. The organizer is ideal for any subject and is useful when differentiating instruction for students needing assistance or for those who need to be challenged.

Using This Graphic Organizer

Model the use of Taking a Bite Out of a Circle Map by having students write topics in the center of the apples. Have students list related information in the outer areas of the apples. The organizer is also an effective tool in small group instruction or independent student use.

The organizer is useful in many other ways:

- Reading: connecting the main idea and details from a text
- Writing: brainstorming ideas for a new writing topic
- Math: relating number sentences to a specific operation
- Science: showing relationships between types of solids or types of liquids
- Social Studies: detailing events around a central theme such as the American Revolution
- Character Education: discussing possible outcomes while having a class discussion on respect

Primary Model

This kindergarten student used Taking a Bite Out of a Circle Map as a pre-assessment for a unit study on people. The student was given the organizer prior to the teaching of the material. Once completed by students, the organizer enabled the teacher to determine how much detail she needed to offer when delivering information.

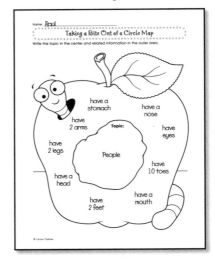

Intermediate Model

This fifth-grade student used Taking a Bite Out of a Circle Map to brainstorm questions he had prior to a research project on the U.S. Reconstruction Era. The organizer allowed the student to gear his research toward what he was most interested in. This streamlined his Internet searches, as well as helped him determine which books he needed to check out from the library.

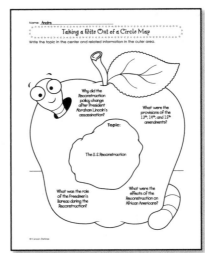

CD-104533 ■ © Carson-Dellosa

Taking a Bite Out of a Circle Map

Write the topic in the center and related information in the outer area.

Topic:

© Carson-Dellosa

Shining a Light on Bright Ideas

Subject Area Uses
- Language Arts
- Social Studies
- Science
- Math

Skills
- Generating ideas
- Collecting and organizing information
- Paraphrasing
- Prewriting

Purpose
Helping students generate ideas and organize and paraphrase information is crucial when preparing them to write effectively. Shining a Light on Bright Ideas is ideal for teaching students how to think critically. The organizer is designed to help students develop writing skills that include sophisticated details, voice, and flow. The organizer, which can be used in whole groups, small groups, or individual workstations, is a valuable tool for differentiating instruction.

Using This Graphic Organizer
Shining a Light on Bright Ideas is an organizer that enables students to be creative. Model the use of the organizer by showing students how to list a topic in the center of the lighthouse and brainstorm related ideas on the rays that stem from it.

The organizer is useful in many other ways:

- Reading: listing and sorting details from a story in a guided reading lesson; paraphrasing information from text
- Writing: serving as a prewriting tool to generate ideas for an original story
- Word Work: creating new words with the same endings
- Social Studies: organizing information from a lesson on the three branches of government
- Science: identifying information learned from a mini-unit on electricity
- Math: Connecting math terminology such as measurement with the various ways in which we measure things (time, length, weight)

Primary Model

This first-grade student chose to use Shining a Light on Bright Ideas as a story web for a how-to writing assignment in which he described how he would build a snowman. The organizer enabled the student to sequence his directions as he listed his ideas.

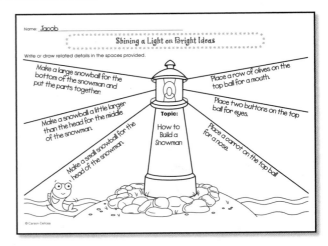

Intermediate Model

This fourth-grade student used Shining a Light on Bright Ideas to organize information he learned about the three branches of the U.S. government. The organizer allowed the student to sort his information for recall and understanding. The student found a use for the additional space on the organizer and used it to explain his understanding of how the three branches of government work together.

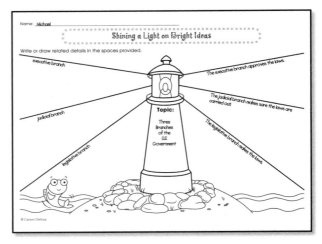

Name: _____

Shining a Light on Bright Ideas

Write or draw related details in the spaces provided.

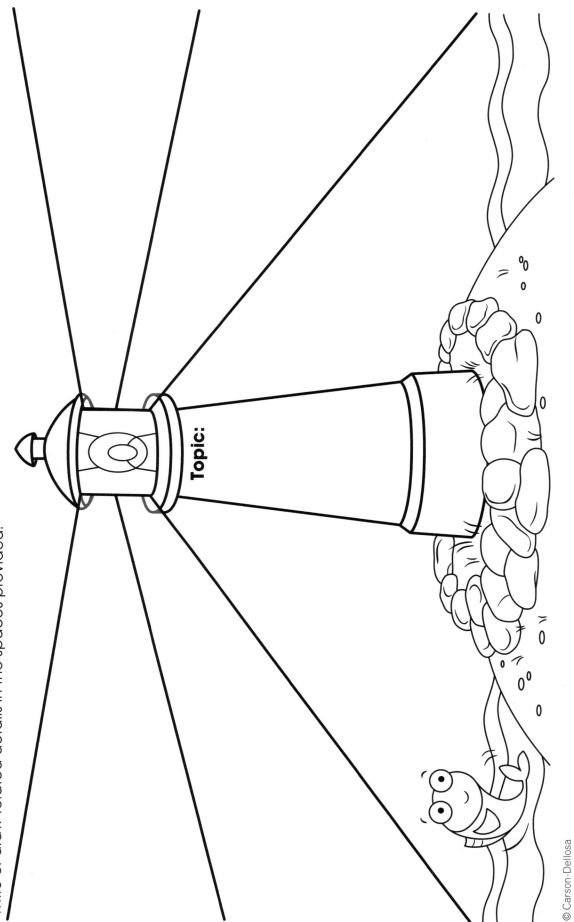

Topic:

© Carson-Dellosa

Composing Connections

Subject Area Uses
- Language Arts
- Science
- Social Studies
- Music

Skills
- Making text-to-self connections
- Organizing and analyzing information
- Understanding and explaining information

Purpose
To help students become discriminating readers, they must first understand how to make connections between what they read and the world around them. Once students are able to make connections to the material they are reading, they can better visualize and understand the text. Composing Connections is designed to help students create and solidify those connections in a visually structured way. The organizer is also a valuable tool to use during music instruction to help students record information about composers, music history, songs, etc.

Using This Graphic Organizer
Connecting information (learned or read) to the world around us is a way to promote comprehension. Model the use of Composing Connections by having students write in the left column what they have learned or read. Have students write or draw what the information in the left column makes them think of.

The organizer is useful in many other ways:

- Reading: connecting to text in an independent workstation or making connections with a book placed in a listening center
- Science: organizing notes and preparing familiar information prior to a formal test
- Social Studies: relating information learned about mapping to the neighborhood around them
- Music: reflecting on an instrumental composition and describing how the music made the students feel

Primary Model

This kindergarten student used Composing Connections in an alphabet center. The student chose letters the class had recently studied and illustrated his understanding of their sounds. The completed organizer became an assessment tool for the teacher, as she was able to see that the student could make connections with his learning.

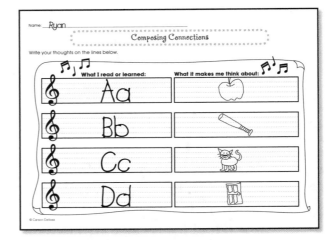

Intermediate Model

This fifth-grade student used Composing Connections for science homework during a unit on health. The student had to record her daily food intake from the food pyramid to analyze her daily nutrition. By using the organizer, the student was able to determine what foods she was lacking and what foods she needed to eat less of to follow a healthful diet.

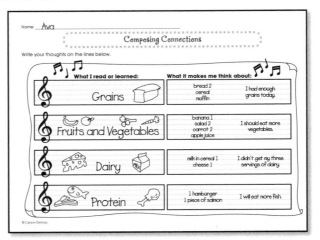

CD-104533 ■ © Carson-Dellosa

Name: _____

Composing Connections

Write your thoughts on the lines below.

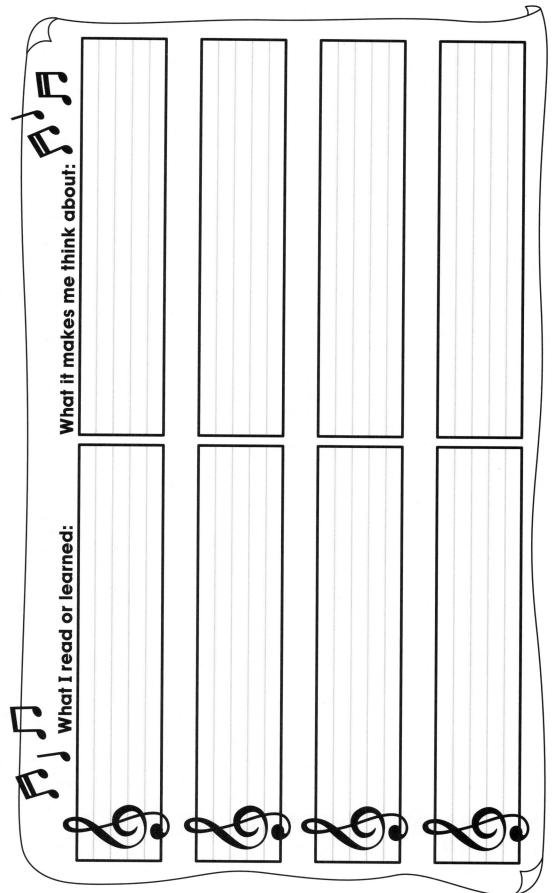

What I read or learned:

What it makes me think about:

© Carson-Dellosa

A Picture Is Worth a Thousand Words

Subject Area Uses
- Language Arts
- Social Studies
- Science
- Math

Skills
- Analyzing details
- Recalling and representing information
- Organizing and summarizing Information
- Prewriting

Purpose
An important skill needed for increased comprehension is the ability to synthesize information from common graphic features. A Picture Is Worth a Thousand Words is an organizer that can help students identify key features in a variety of texts. The organizer has a multitude of uses across the curriculum, from sequencing information to analyzing details from a text. The organizer is also ideal for use during one-on-one instruction, in small groups, or as a whole-class activity.

Using This Graphic Organizer
The pictures organized on A Picture Is Worth a Thousand Words prompt students to examine information, summarize content, and organize material. The organizer is also perfect for differentiation because it allows students to write or draw what they have learned.

The organizer is useful in many other ways:

- Reading: examining details from nonfiction texts where students label specific graphic features (headings, subheadings, captions, titles, or bold or italicized words), sequencing events or detailing character changes from a guided reading story
- Writing: brainstorming to find prewriting ideas for new stories or cartoon strips
- Word Study: providing examples of nouns, verbs, adjectives, or adverbs
- Social Studies: organizing, sequencing, and summarizing information learned about the early settlers
- Math: representing fact families and reflecting on their relationships

Primary Model

This kindergarten student used A Picture Is Worth a Thousand Words in science class after his teacher read the story *The Seasons* by Ian Smith (Qed Publishing, 2005). The student illustrated each of the seasons as an assessment so that his teacher would know what he learned from the story. The student used the last picture to describe his favorite season and tell why he liked it so much.

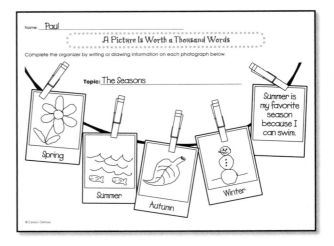

Intermediate Model

This fifth-grade student used a Picture Is Worth a Thousand Words in social studies class while reading a chapter from *First Pass Under Heaven: One Man's 4,000- Kilometre Trek Along the Great Wall of China* by Nathan Hoturoa Gray (Penguin Global, 2006). The student was able to recall information from her reading and organize it in detail. By using the organizer, the student became more familiar with the use of graphic features and how using them can help her recall information.

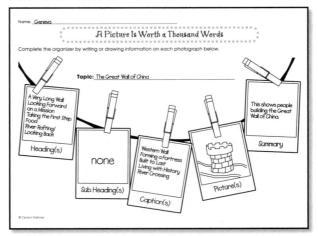

CD-104533 ■ © Carson-Dellosa

Name: _____

A Picture Is Worth a Thousand Words

Complete the organizer by writing or drawing information on each photograph below.

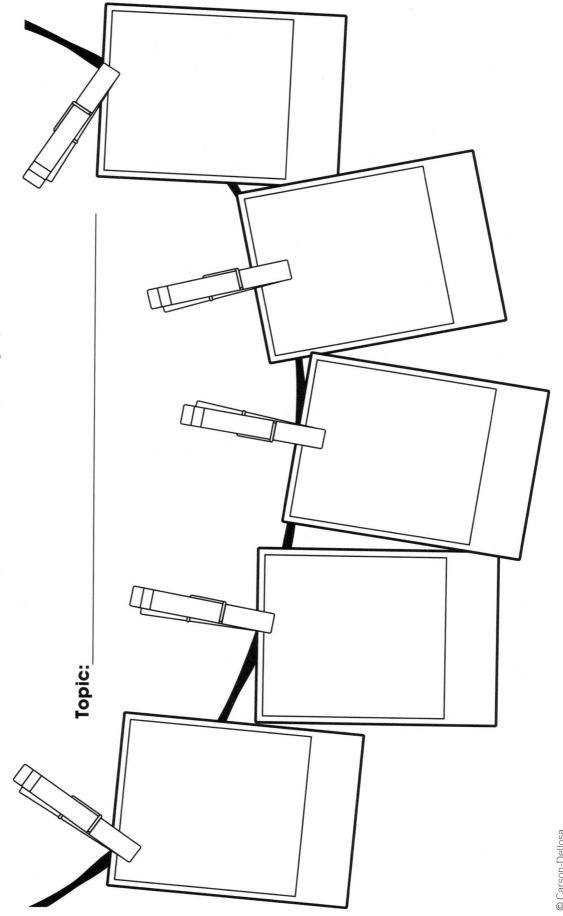

Topic: _____

© Carson-Dellosa

Inspecting for Evidence

Subject Area Uses
- Language Arts
- Science
- Social Studies
- Math
- Character Education

Skills
- Locating and analyzing details
- Sequencing information
- Justifying answers

Purpose
Active engagement in the classroom is achieved when students are required to provide evidence for their thinking. Inspecting for Evidence is designed to provide a structure for students to analyze details, form opinions, and justify answers with evidence. By using the organizer, students are able to paint pictures of their learning while simultaneously providing a visual tool for learning assessment.

Using This Graphic Organizer
Model the use of Inspecting for Evidence by placing a large copy on the board. Explain to students how to form opinions and make predictions or provide a fact on the topic line of the organizer while writing statements in the shoes. Then, write facts in the spyglasses to model justifying answers.

The organizer is useful in many other ways:

- Reading: describing characters from a guided reading lesson or a book used in a listening center
- Science: explaining why specific steps in an experiment do not work
- Social Studies: listing information about historical figures and what roles they played in history
- Math: illustrating math problems with pictures and number sentences
- Character Education: describing characteristics about classmates to begin a class discussion

Primary Model
This second-grade student used Inspecting for Evidence during a language arts lesson as pre-assessment before doing a study on character analysis. Before teaching, the teacher had students make statements about friends or family. She then asked students to justify their statements with facts about each person they listed. By using the organizer, this student learned how to find factual information that would support his thinking.

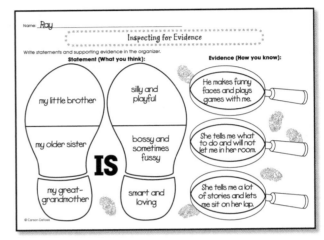

Intermediate Model
This fourth-grade student used Inspecting for Evidence during a science lesson on rocks and minerals. The student had to analyze each item, describe it, and provide proof for her thinking. By using the organizer, the student had a clearer understanding of rocks and minerals and was better prepared for an upcoming quiz on the subject.

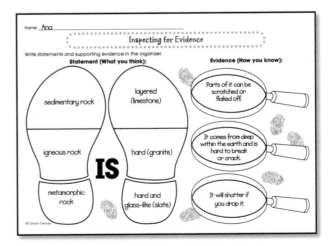

CD-104533 ■ © Carson-Dellosa

Name: _____

Inspecting for Evidence

Write statements and supporting evidence in the organizer.

Statement (What you think):

Evidence (How you know):

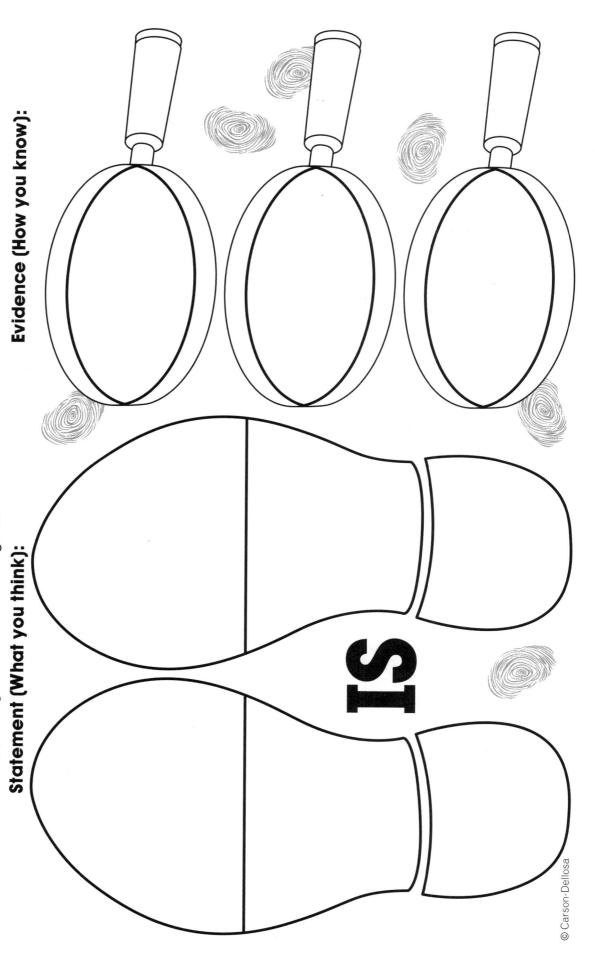

IS

© Carson-Dellosa

Coat of Arms

Subject Area Uses
- Language Arts
- Social Studies
- Math

Skills
- Organizing information
- Recalling and summarizing details

Purpose
Identifying key details is critical to developing true understanding of material. Coat of Arms is an organizer that helps students take details and organize them in ways that are visually structured. Once it is viewed as a whole rather than in separate sections, the organizer then becomes a representation of material learned. It works well in many subject areas. And, because students can complete the organizer with words or drawings, it is suited to students of all ages and ability levels.

Using This Graphic Organizer
Model the use of Coat of Arms by writing information related to a topic, a place, or a figure in each section. Then, demonstrate how each piece is critical to the learning as a whole.

The organizer is useful in many other ways:

- Reading: identifying characteristics of a character from a story or identifying details about the setting of a story
- Social Studies: illustrating details about a geographic location or a key historical figure
- Math: describing attributes of three-dimensional figures

Primary Model

This kindergarten student used Coat of Arms to describe herself. By including details about what she likes to eat, where she likes to go, what her hobbies are, and what she loves the most, she is able to create a visual representation of what makes her unique.

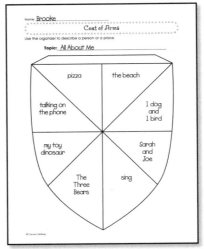

Intermediate Model

This fifth-grade student used Coat of Arms in social studies to record information he learned about Ronald Reagan. By sorting the information into different sections, the student was able to become more familiar with the historical figure and use the organizer as a study tool before an oral presentation.

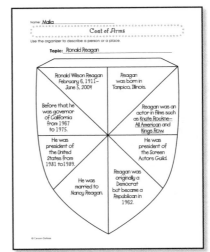

Name: _____

Coat of Arms

Use the organizer to describe a person or a place.

Topic:_____

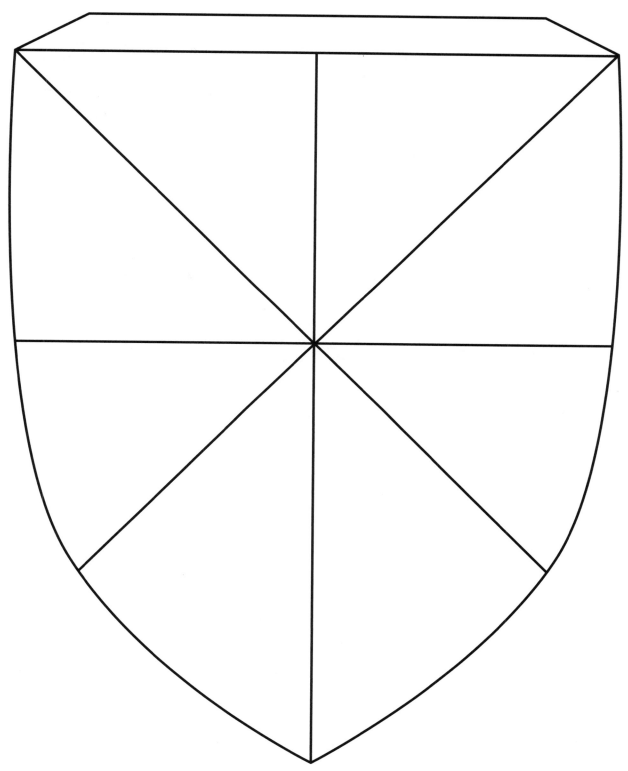

© Carson-Dellosa

Subject Area Uses
- Language Arts
- Social Studies
- Science

Skills
- Organizing information
- Writing with purpose
- Recalling and summarizing details
- Planning

Purpose
Organizing information is important when writing. Pieces of a Puzzle is an organizer that is visually structured to enable students to see that a good written piece should have a beginning, a middle, and an end. The organizer also helps students see the importance of details within the body of a written piece by formatting three areas within the structure dedicated to details only. By using the Pieces of a Puzzle organizer, students can develop competency in writing organized, original, and refined written pieces.

Using This Graphic Organizer
Model the use of Pieces of a Puzzle in a whole-group, small-group, or individual setting by having students write beginnings at the top of their organizers, related details in the three middle pieces, and conclusions at the bottom. The visual pattern will help students see that when the pieces are put together, they form a fully developed piece.

The organizer is useful in many other ways:

- Reading: placing story events in order from a story read aloud or from books selected for independent reading
- Writing: organizing information for a writing assignment
- Social Studies: demonstrating part-whole connections such as describing the events that led to the Vietnam War
- Science: planning steps for an assignment or a project on weather

Primary Model

This first-grade student used Pieces of a Puzzle as a tool when asked to write a paragraph about his pet dog. By using the organizer, the student was able to clearly understand that a good story has a beginning, a middle, and an end. The organizer served as the first step in the writing process and as a conferencing tool for the teacher and the student to review before he started a rough draft.

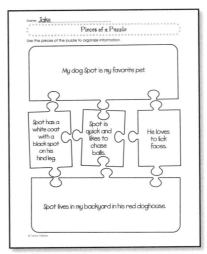

Intermediate Model

This fifth-grade student used Pieces of a Puzzle to write a persuasive essay about a service-learning project he completed for science class. The student easily connected his introductory paragraph to his concluding paragraph and understood that details were integral to the body of the essay. By including all of the pieces, the student wrote a coherent and well-thought-out essay.

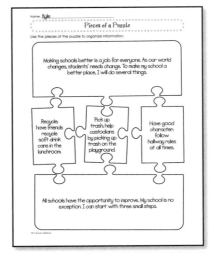

 CD-104533 ■ © Carson-Dellosa

Name: _____

Pieces of a Puzzle

Use the pieces of the puzzle to organize information.

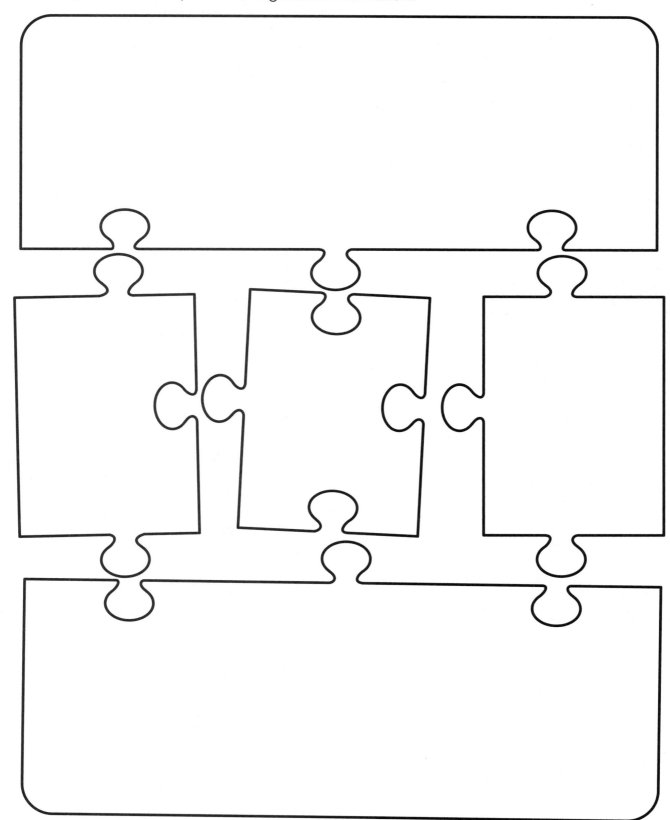

© Carson-Dellosa

Spinning Summaries

Subject Area Uses
- Language Arts
- Social Studies
- Science

Skills
- Summarizing information
- Narrowing topics or research ideas
- Paraphrase information

Purpose

Summarizing information can be difficult for some students. Being able to determine the most important information within a text and narrow it down to the most important details is a tool that can help students with comprehension. Spinning Summaries mimics an inverted triangle and is designed to help students understand the narrowing process. By using the organizer, students will be better equipped to develop strategies to paraphrase information and extract key elements from within a topic, as well as relate learned information to their worlds by answering the question in the smaller top.

Using This Graphic Organizer

The Spinning Summaries organizer has an ideal shape for summarizing. Model the use of the organizer on the board by placing a broad topic in the handle of the spinning top. Ask students to narrow the topic on each line thereafter until they have reached a focused idea.

The organizer is useful in many other ways:

- Reading: summarizing information from a selected text
- Writing: narrowing a topic for an original writing assignment or detailing information for a personal narrative
- Science: narrowing steps for a research project while working with a group

Primary Model

This first-grade student used Spinning Summaries during reading time to summarize *Cool Time Song* by Carole Lexa Schaefer (Viking Juvenile, 2005). The organizer helped the student retrieve important details and organize the information for better understanding.

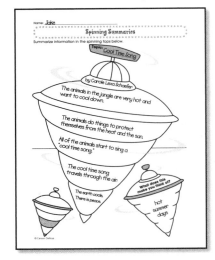

Intermediate Model

This fifth-grade student used Spinning Summaries to paraphrase information he read about lizards in science class. By using the organizer, the student was able to narrow learned information and discover that the Gila monster is not only an interesting lizard but is also of interest to the medical community.

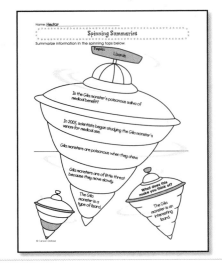

CD-104533 ■ © Carson-Dellosa

Name: _____

Spinning Summaries

Summarize information in the spinning tops below.

Topic:

What does this make you think of?

© Carson-Dellosa

Subject Area Uses

- All subject areas

Skills

- Writing with purpose
- Organizing information
- Using details

Purpose

Learning to write properly is important for all students and is essential across the curriculum. Many students lack the ability to develop content and give solid structure to their writing. Writing Around the World is organized in a way that helps students prepare introductions, body content, and conclusions for their writing. By using the organizer, students will better understand how the introductory parts of a paper and the concluding remarks are related, as well as how they should develop the body content with deliberate and connecting details.

Using This Graphic Organizer

Model the use of Writing Around the World by placing a large copy on the board. Ask students to help choose a topic and write an introductory sentence or paragraph about the topic, detail sentences, and a concluding sentence to connect to the introduction.

The organizer is useful in many other ways:

- Reading: retelling a story read in class
- Writing: brainstorming for an original writing piece or as a template for a final draft
- Social Studies: writing a letter as if the student were a historical figure such as a president who was addressing his cabinet
- Science: summarizing findings after an experiment or paraphrasing information from a research report on a famous scientist
- Math: describing steps to solve a division problem or to find the amount of miles or kilometers between two locations
- Character Education: serving as a reflection tool where students describe the reactions they might have to a particular situation

Primary Model

This first-grade student used Writing Around the World to plan his final draft during a social studies lesson on community helpers. The teacher asked students to write about the people that work in the surrounding area. By using the organizer, the student gained a better understanding of the roles that community helpers play, as well as learned how to structure his writing so that it includes an introduction, a body, and a conclusion.

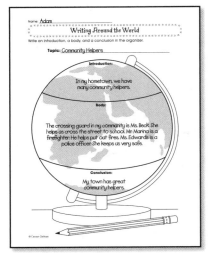

Intermediate Model

This third-grade student used Writing Around the World in language arts class after returning from a school break. The student wrote about what he and his family did during the break. By using the organizer, the student was able to organize his thinking in a structured way that showed a clear connection between his introductory sentence and his conclusion.

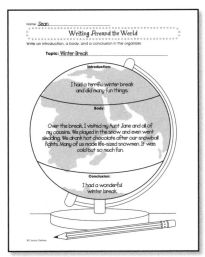

Name: _____

Writing Around the World

Write an introduction, a body, and a conclusion in the organizer.

Topic: _____

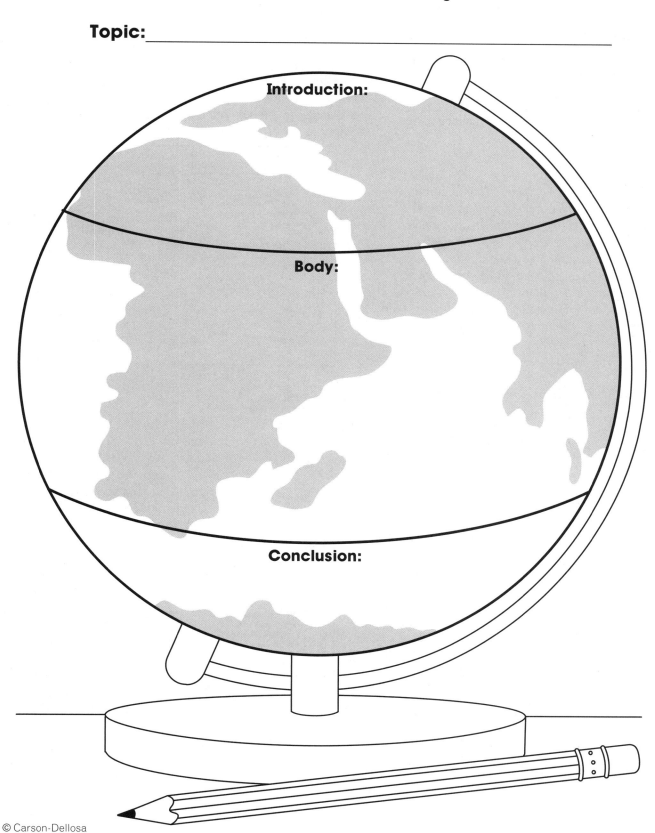

Introduction:

Body:

Conclusion:

© Carson-Dellosa

Don't Judge a Book by Its Cover

Subject Area Uses
- Language Arts
- Literary texts in Social Studies
- Character Education

Skills
- Summarizing book reports
- Recalling and organizing information
- Reflecting on and analyzing information

Purpose
Writing book reports can be fun for students. Book reports are excellent tools for assessing students' abilities to summarize and analyze details effectively. Don't Judge a Book by Its Cover allows students to identify and analyze key points from a selected text and summarize the plot and the conclusion. The organizer ensures that students use critical thinking skills, as well as asks them to rate their texts.

Using This Graphic Organizer
Don't Judge a Book by Its Cover is a structured book report template to use in all subject areas and with students of varied ability levels.

The organizer is useful in many other ways:

- Reading: recalling information read from a fiction or nonfiction piece of literature read in class or at home
- Social Studies: reflecting on a historical fiction text used in a guided reading lesson about the Boston Tea Party
- Character Education: serving as a reflection tool after reading a book on showing good character such as *The Meanest Thing to Say: A Little Bill Book for Beginning Readers* by Bill Cosby (Cartwheel, 1997).

Primary Model

This first-grade student used Don't Judge a Book by Its Cover for a homework assignment to retell a story the teacher read in class. The book was entitled *Llama Llama Mad at Mama* by Anna Dewdney (Viking Juvenile, 2007). After beginning the organizer at school and then finishing at home, the student was able to organize the information read earlier in the day. Later, the organizer served as an assessment tool for the teacher.

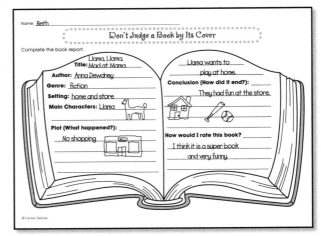

Intermediate Model

This fifth-grade student used Don't Judge a Book by Its Cover while working with a partner in social studies class. The organizer served as a tool for the students to summarize the story *The Real Benedict Arnold* by Jim Murphy (Clarion Books, 2007), a book selected based on their reading levels. The organizer helped the students recall and retell information learned from the text.

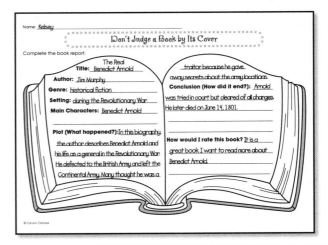

Name: _____

Don't Judge a Book by Its Cover

Complete the book report.

Title: _____

Author: _____

Genre: _____

Setting: _____

Main Characters: _____

Plot (What happened?): _____

Conclusion (How did it end?): _____

How would I rate this book? _____

© Carson-Dellosa

The Daily Times

Subject Area Uses
- Language Arts
- Social Studies

Skills
- Summarizing informational text
- Organizing and analyzing information
- Sequencing
- Making judgments

Purpose
Using nonfiction text to teach students is a best practice that prepares students for test taking, solid comprehension, and daily skills. The Daily Times organizer helps students summarize key features from informational text and evaluate their purpose. By organizing information in a well-formatted structure, students are able to put together the pieces of an event or a topic to fully understand its meaning or impact.

Using This Graphic Organizer
The Daily Times is an ideal tool for students to use in combination with informational text or personal events. Model the use of the organizer by showing students how to locate the information for each section. The Daily Times then extends learning by evaluating the importance of the story and how or if it changed people.

The organizer is useful in many other ways:

- Reading: understanding and identifying key pieces of information in text
- Writing: documenting information from a personal event or a recent school event such as the 100th day of school
- Social Studies: researching information from a newspaper, a magazine, a Web article, or a TV news report or for homework or a class assignment

Primary Model

This second-grade student used The Daily Times during a unit on fairy tales. The school put on a production of *Cinderella* in the auditorium. As a culminating activity, the student had to pretend to be a newspaper writer on assignment after the prince's ball. By using the organizer, the student was able to determine what information goes into the writing of a news article. It also helped him organize his information and pick out key details.

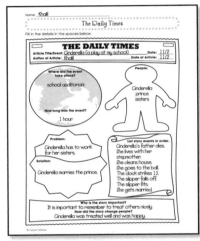

Intermediate Model

This fifth-grade student used The Daily Times in social studies class to review current events. The student chose an article from the newspaper about volunteers who came together to help repair some homes in a local neighborhood. The organizer helped the student learn how to read for details and understand how each detail is important to the overall story.

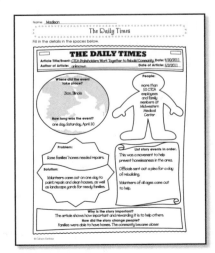

CD-104533 ■ © Carson-Dellosa

Name: _____

Fill in the details in the spaces below.

THE DAILY TIMES

Article Title/Event: _____ **Date:** _____
Author of Article: _____ **Date of Article:** _____

Where did the event take place?

How long was the event?

People:

Problem:

Solution:

List story events in order.

Why is the story important?

How did the story change people?

© Carson-Dellosa

Wordy Wagons

Subject Area Uses
- Language Arts
- Social Studies
- Science
- Literary texts in all subject areas

Skills
- Sequencing—beginning, middle, end
- Identifying parts of a story
- Brainstorming
- Summarizing
- Prewriting

Purpose
Arranging events in order is important in all subject areas and is critical to the understanding of story structure. Wordy Wagons is a simplistic and useful tool that helps students identify the specific parts of a story, prewrite short stories, or summarize information. The organizer is also a differentiation tool to use in a writing station or as an individual intervention for a student who is in the beginning stages of a written piece.

Using This Graphic Organizer
Model the use of Wordy Wagons by placing a large copy on the board and walking students through a step-by-step process of placing the beginning, the middle, and the end of a story in the designated wagon.

The organizer is useful in many other ways:

- Reading: recalling information from a story read aloud, in a guided reading station, or independently at home
- Writing: serving as a prewriting tool to sequence the steps a student takes to get to school in the morning or as a template for an original written piece
- Social Studies: summarizing a story read or an event that has happened in the news
- Science: recording steps taken during an experiment

Primary Model

This first-grade student used Wordy Wagons to retell the events from the story *The Missing Tooth* by Christianne C. Jones (Picture Window Books, 2006). By drawing and describing the story events in order, the student was able to demonstrate his understanding of the events in the story.

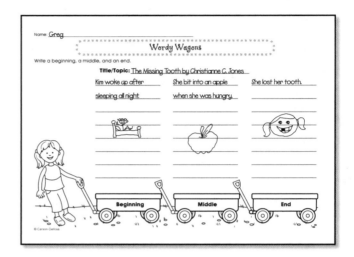

Intermediate Model

This fifth-grade student used Wordy Wagons in science class to record her work on a scientific experiment involving vinegar and baking soda. By placing her work on the organizer, the student was able to record, retell, and review the steps she took.

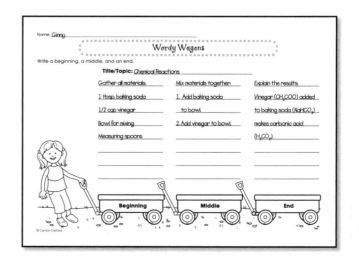

CD-104533 ■ © Carson-Dellosa

Name: _____

Wordy Wagons

Write a beginning, a middle, and an end.

Title/Topic: _____

Beginning   Middle   End

© Carson-Dellosa

Tickets Back in Time

Subject Area Uses
- Language Arts
- Social Studies

Skills
- Sequencing information in a time line
- Identifying key events and details
- Ordering and arranging information

Purpose
Identifying key elements and arranging information in chronological order are useful skills for students as they investigate the structure of a story. The use of a visual organizer with text helps students of all levels isolate key events and pieces of information. Tickets Back in Time is a four-step organizer that guides students to sequencing events. The organizer is also an effective tool that helps students understand action-reaction and causal relationships.

Using This Graphic Organizer
Model the use of Tickets Back in Time by telling students to write their information in the numbered boxes in order. Have students begin writing their information in Ticket 1 and progress to Ticket 4 by placing sequential information in each.

The organizer is useful in many other ways:

- Reading: recalling events from a text of any genre while working in a guided reading group
- Writing: serving as a prewriting tool or as a template for primary writing
- Social Studies: sequencing the events that led up to the Great Depression or identifying key events in a student's life (to be completed at home with a parent or a guardian)

Primary Model

This first-grade student used Tickets Back in Time to create a time line of his life. The student listed the events in the tickets, which allowed him to have an organized representation that helped him when he presented his information to the class.

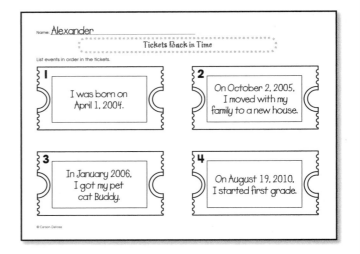

Intermediate Model

This fourth-grade student used Tickets Back in Time in social studies class to create a time line on U.S. President Barack Obama's life using an article he read previously. By writing the information in the organizer, the student was able to see what steps President Obama took to achieve his presidency. The organizer also served as an assessment tool for the teacher the following day.

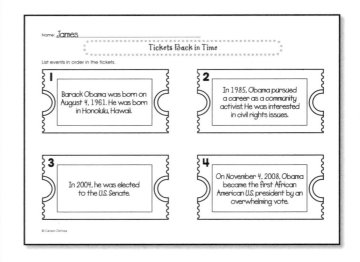

CD-104533 ■ © Carson-Dellosa

Name: _____

Tickets Back in Time

List events in order in the tickets.

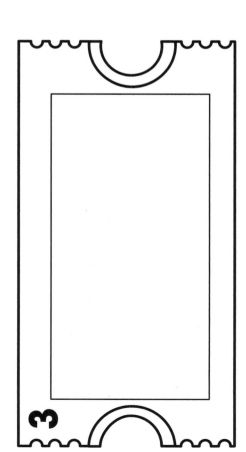

© Carson-Dellosa

Fast-Track Flowchart

Subject Area Uses
- Language Arts
- Science
- Social Studies
- Math

Skills
- Sequencing with ordinal numbers
- Understanding processes
- Organizing information

Purpose
Sequencing information in a specific order teaches students the importance of structure. As students sequence, they develop the skills to interpret and explain how altering steps can change an outcome. The Fast-Track Flowchart is ideal for helping students sequence using ordinal numbers. The flowchart is a valuable organizational tool that uses a sequential, step-by-step process.

Using This Graphic Organizer
The Fast-Track Flowchart is designed in a circular pattern and divided into six numbered sections. Model the use of the organizer by placing it on the board and demonstrating how to put things in order as they occur, beginning with step one.

The organizer is useful in many other ways:

- Reading: retelling a story from a guided reading lesson and placing events in sequential order
- Writing: arranging information during a whole-group writing lesson where students describe the steps for getting ready for school in the morning
- Science: listing the steps in a scientific investigation
- Math: explaining the steps for long division in a homework assignment
- Social Studies: detailing specific directions from students' homes to the school

Primary Model

This third-grade student used Fast-Track Flowchart during a writing lesson when asked to describe how to make a peanut butter and jelly sandwich. By using the organizer and placing her information in a series of steps, she was able to visualize and understand the placement of each step and how the sequencing of each step was critical to her writing.

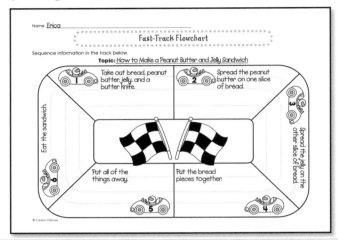

Intermediate Model

This fifth-grade student used Fast-Track Flowchart during a science lesson about recalling steps taken. The use of the organizer allowed the student to revisit the science process to determine if the steps he took were accurate, sequential, and important.

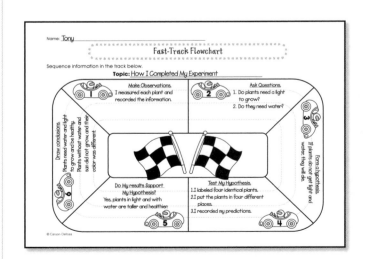

Name: _____

Fast-Track Flowchart

Sequence information in the track below.

Topic: _____

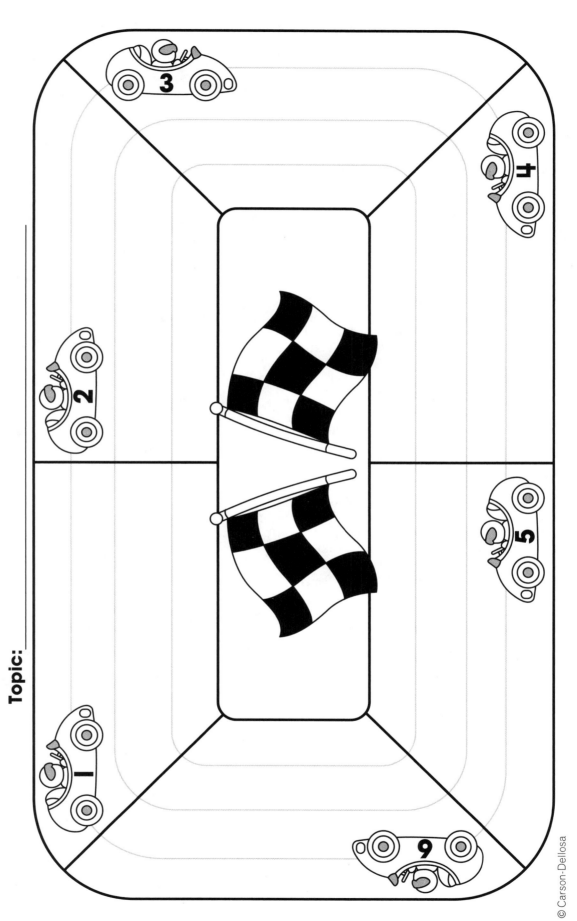

© Carson-Dellosa

Get Your Ducks in a Row

Subject Area Uses
- Language Arts
- Math
- Science
- Social Studies

Skills
- Sequencing with ordinal words
- Following directions
- Giving directions

Purpose
Sequencing events and information is an important skill for students to understand and use in all subject areas. Typically, students use number references when placing things in order but often do not have the opportunity to practice using ordinal words. Get Your Ducks in a Row is a tool that allows students to practice number words while working with chronological material. By using the organizer, students become proficient in using ordinal words to describe sequential events. The organizer is ideal to use across the curriculum and with varied ability levels.

Using This Graphic Organizer
Model the use of Get Your Ducks in a Row by having students write the first step to a process in the puddle listed as "first." Have students proceed to follow the second, third, and last ducks with the corresponding information.

The organizer is useful in many other ways:

- Reading: sequencing events from a teacher-read or independent selection
- Writing: detailing information in a how-to writing assignment
- Science: ordering specific tasks in a hands-on experiment with a small group
- Math: giving directions for completing a multi-step word problem
- Social Studies: explaining events that led up to the Cold War

Primary Model

This second-grade student used Get Your Ducks in a Row at a writing center to describe the steps for cleaning his room. By placing the events in order in the organizer, the student was able to understand the importance of following the steps of a procedure, as well as understand the importance of using ordinal words in his writing.

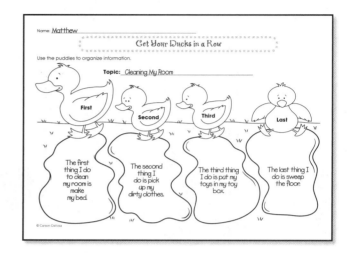

Intermediate Model

This fourth-grade student used Get Your Ducks in a Row in math class for teacher assessment. The student was asked to describe the steps for solving double-digit division problems. By having the student explain the steps in order, the teacher was able to determine if she understood the process completely.

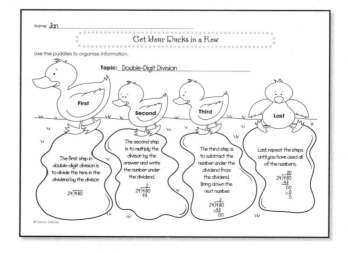

CD-104533 ■ © Carson-Dellosa

Name: _____

Get Your Ducks in a Row

Use the puddles to organize information.

Topic: _____

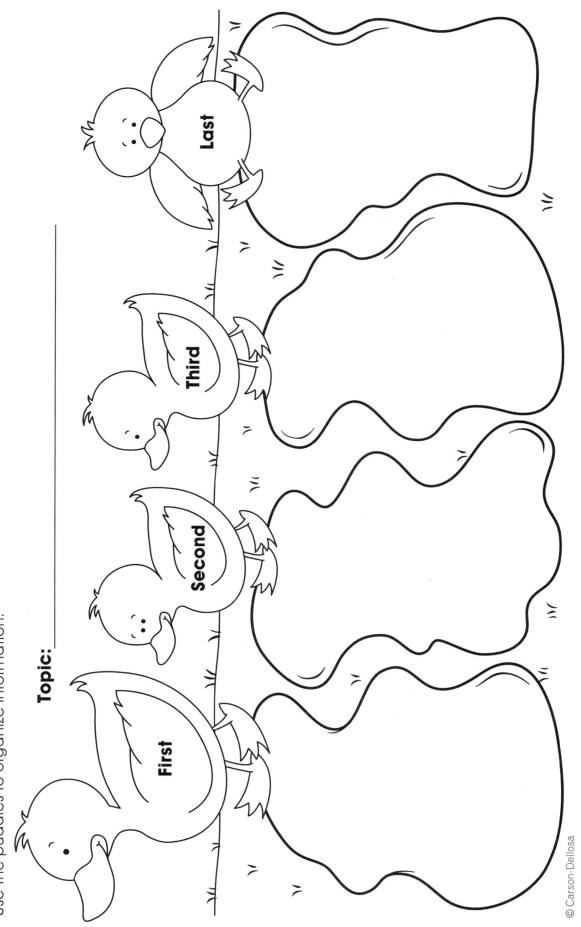

First

Second

Third

Last

© Carson-Dellosa

Stepping Through a Storyboard

Subject Area Uses
- Language Arts
- Social Studies
- Science

Skills
- Sequencing with storyboards
- Organizing information
- Analyzing and organizing events

Purpose
Being able to sequence information is important in all subject areas. Stepping Through a Storyboard is designed to help students of all ability levels organize information. The organizer provides opportunities for students to analyze events for importance, as well as arrange them chronologically. This practice allows students to explore information within content to later discuss in small groups. When students are able to analyze and discuss the information, reading comprehension improves.

Using This Graphic Organizer
Stepping Through a Storyboard provides a visually engaging format for sequencing information. Model the use of the organizer by placing a large copy on the board and walking students through a simple story as they describe the events in order.

The organizer is useful in many other ways:

- Reading: organizing the events of a story read in a guided reading lesson
- Writing: organizing information in writing as a prewriting strategy to be discussed later in a writing conference
- Social Studies: sequencing information taken from a biography that displays the life and times of a famous baseball player
- Science: analyzing and organizing a series of events in an experiment that showcases how each step is important to the end product

Primary Model

This second-grade student used Stepping Through a Storyboard to record the events from a book she read in her reading group. The book was entitled *Miss Ellie's Turban* by Ellen V. Rauh (Xlibris, 2010). By using the organizer, the student was able to place the events from the story in order and summarize what happened using the important details.

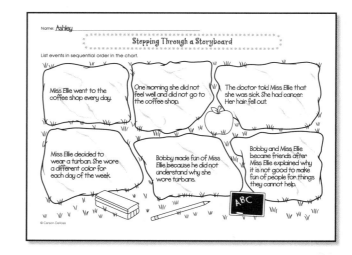

Intermediate Model

This fifth-grade student used Stepping Through a Storyboard to record the life events of Arthur Ashe. By using the organizer, the student was able to analyze and choose the important events from the famous tennis player's life that led him to Wimbledon.

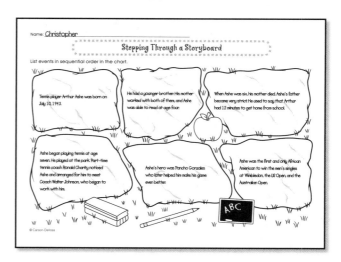

 © Carson-Dellosa

Name: _____

Stepping Through a Storyboard

List events in sequential order in the chart.

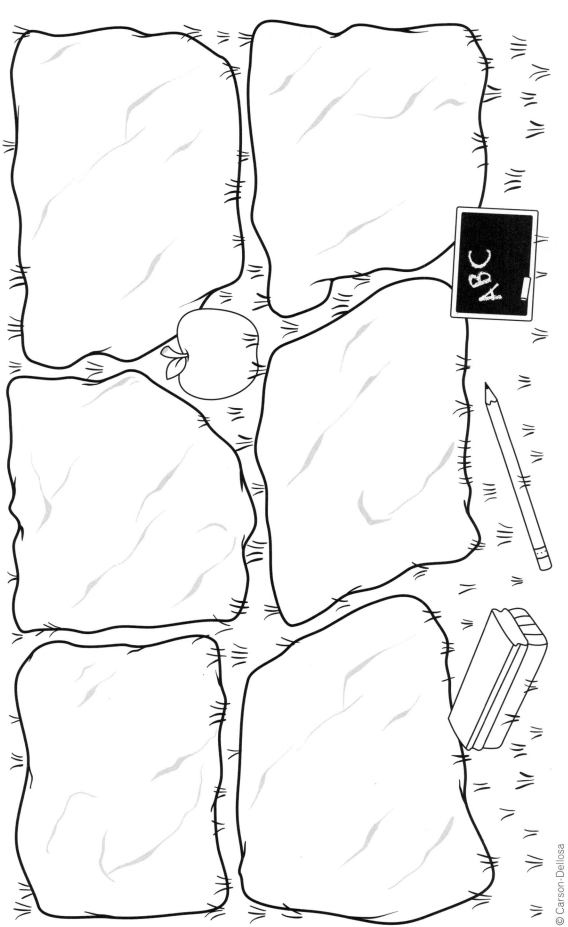

© Carson-Dellosa

Circling Through a Cycle

Subject Area Uses
- Language Arts
- Science
- Social Studies
- Character Education

Skills
- Sequencing with cycles
- Observing and recording
- Summarizing and paraphrasing
- Recalling events

Purpose
Cycle organizers enable students to recall, order, and understand sequential steps in a process. Circling Through a Cycle helps students understand that every process has a beginning, a middle, and an end and is continual. The organizer is applicable in all subject areas and with students of varied ability levels.

Using This Graphic Organizer
Circling Through a Cycle is ideal for students observing the various stages of an event. Model the use of the organizer by having students use it as an assessment tool after a lesson on the life cycle of a butterfly.

The organizer is useful in many other ways:

- Reading: detailing events from a selected text
- Writing: recording steps for a how-to paper on the steps of brushing your teeth
- Science: recording the process used during a group experiment or explaining the various stages of an animal's development
- Social Studies: summarizing the events that led up to the design of the American flag
- Character Education: listing the events that might take place if a student did not tell the truth and detailing how one lie might lead to another

Primary Model

This kindergarten student used Circling Through a Cycle in a science lesson to record the life cycle of a butterfly. By using the organizer, the student was able to order the events and understand how each step played a part in the next.

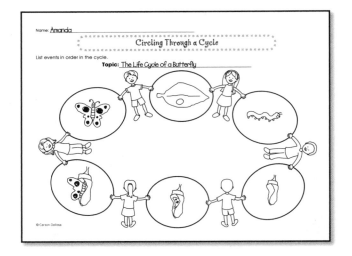

Intermediate Model

This fifth-grade student used Circling Through a Cycle in social studies class to record the steps leading up to the election of a new president in the United States. By placing the events in order, the student learned about the process of elections and how the process repeats itself every four years.

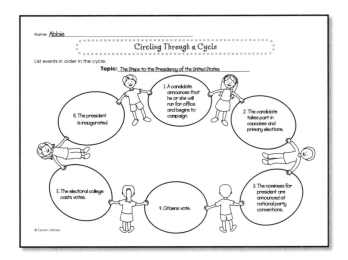

 CD-104533 ■ © Carson-Dellosa

Circling Through a Cycle

List events in order in the cycle.

Topic: _____

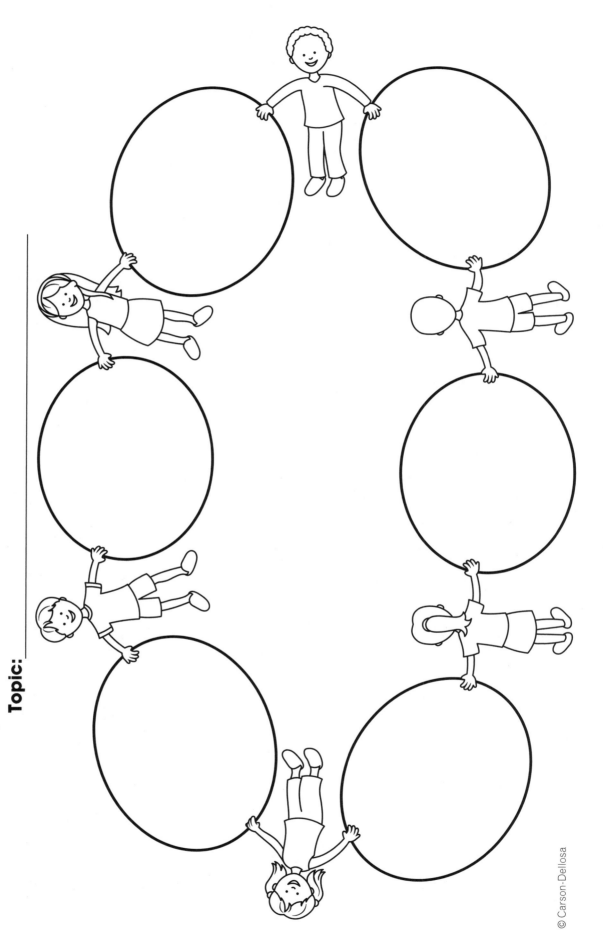

© Carson-Dellosa

Riding a Chain of Events

Subject Area Uses
- Language Arts
- Science
- Social Studies
- Character Education

Skills
- Sequencing through a chain of events
- Tracking information
- Evaluating events in a cycle
- Identifying cause and effect

Purpose
Placing information on a chain of events organizer helps create a visual representation of how one event becomes dependent on another. Riding a Chain of Events is a tool that enables students to place events in sequential order and to reflect on the events' causal relationships. When students understand how to prioritize or place information in a sequential chart, it allows them to recognize how they can change the outcome by changing the preceding events.

Using This Graphic Organizer
Most stories have a definite sequence of events. When students are able to discuss events and list events in the order that they took place, students are better equipped to reevaluate their actions and make informed decisions. Students who know how to organize information can better understand their reading assignments and will be more successful readers.

The organizer is useful in many other ways:

- Reading: listing and reflecting on the events from a selected piece of literature
- Writing: creating an original written piece to describe how studying and paying attention in class can lead to good grades
- Social Studies: sequencing and then analyzing information on the life of a famous American
- Science: explaining steps in a process when completing an experiment on making solids from liquids
- Character Education: tracking information leading to an event and making decisions about how the situation could have been handled differently

Primary Model

This first-grade student used Riding a Chain of Events during a lesson on honesty. The student reflected on the topic of stealing after being read a story in which one student takes a pencil from another. The organizer helped the student see the possibilities of what could happen and how different actions can lead to different reactions.

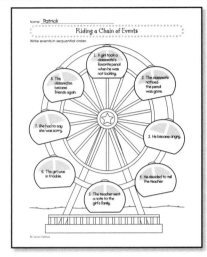

Intermediate Model

This fifth-grade student used Riding a Chain of Events in social studies class while working with a small group led by a parent volunteer. The student learned about the events that led up to the death of Dr. Martin Luther King Jr. Placing the events in order in the organizer helped the student see the contributions of the famous American and how the United States came to celebrate a day in his honor.

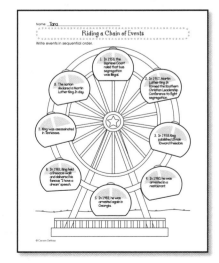

CD-104533 © Carson-Dellosa

Name: _____

Riding a Chain of Events

Write events in sequential order.

© Carson-Dellosa

Royal Rankings

Subject Area Uses

- Language Arts
- Social Studies
- Science
- Character Education

Skills

- Ranking and prioritizing
- Ordering in a series
- Listing steps in a process

Purpose

The use of ranking and prioritizing is beneficial in any academic or social setting and throughout life. The Royal Rankings organizer enables students to learn how to analyze priorities and discriminate between what is most important. By using the organizer, students will become more proficient at making decisions and at weighing, ranking, and analyzing information.

Using This Graphic Organizer

Model the use of Royal Rankings by having students list items in the organizer from the most important to the least. The organizer provides an area for explanation to require students to use higher-order thinking skills.

The organizer is useful in many other ways:

- Writing: listing the steps of the writing process and explaining why each step is important for leading to the next step
- Social Studies: listing military rankings in order and explaining the hierarchal position of each
- Science: listing the food groups that students need to eat the most of and why
- Character Education: ranking and prioritizing rules as students review classroom procedures and why they are followed in a specific order

Primary Model

This second-grade student used Royal Rankings along with her teacher to list the steps of the writing process. By using the organizer, the student could see the order and the importance of each step.

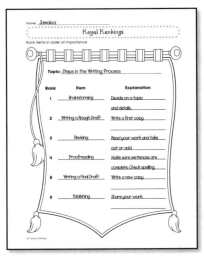

Intermediate Model

This fourth-grade student used Royal Rankings in science class while studying the six types of simple machines that make work easier. By using the organizer, the student was able to list the six simple machines in order of importance in his life. The student also discovered that many everyday objects around us are good examples of simple machines.

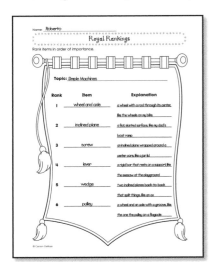

CD-104533　© Carson-Dellosa

Name: _____

Royal Rankings

Rank items in order of importance.

Topic: _____

Rank	Item	Explanation
1	_____	_____
2	_____	_____
3	_____	_____
4	_____	_____
5	_____	_____
6	_____	_____

© Carson-Dellosa

What Is My Question? Find the Answer

Subject Area Uses
- Language Arts
- Science
- Social Studies
- Math

Skills
- Questioning
- Investigating and researching
- Organizing and analyzing information

Purpose

What Is My Question? Find the Answer is designed to help students develop independent questioning techniques. The organizer strengthens students' strategies for understanding different levels of questions, from simple recall to more complex questions. Designed for use before, during, and after instruction, the organizer allows students to place their questions about their topics on the organizer to guide learning and list questions they have during instruction.

Using This Graphic Organizer

Reading comprehension is amplified when students are able to choose topics they want to learn about and to structure their own learning experiences by researching what they want to know. After students list their topics, have them write their questions in the top of the question marks. After instruction or research, have students record their answers in the bottom portion of the question marks.

The organizer is useful in many other ways:

- Reading: recording questions and answers about the main character of a book before and after reading or responding to narrative elements of a story
- Science: recording questions about a topic prior to an experiment
- Social Studies: asking and answering questions about historical figures or guiding learning during an independent research project
- Math: listing questions about a new unit of study on geometry or any math-related topic

Primary Model

This second-grade student used What Is My Question? Find the Answer when asked to take a picture walk through an informational text on snakes. The student then used the organizer while reading to record any additional questions he had. By writing his questions ahead of time, the student knew what to listen and look for.

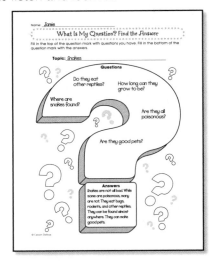

Intermediate Model

This fourth-grade student used What Is My Question? Find the Answer in social studies class to design a research project on Francis Marion. The organizer enabled the student to narrow her research ahead of time, as well as summarize her learning at the end of the project.

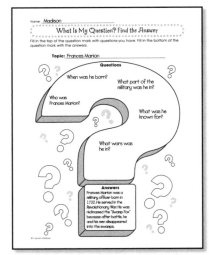

CD-104533 ■ © Carson-Dellosa

Name: _____

What Is My Question? Find the Answer

Fill in the top of the question mark with questions you have. Fill in the bottom of the question mark with the answers.

Topic: _____

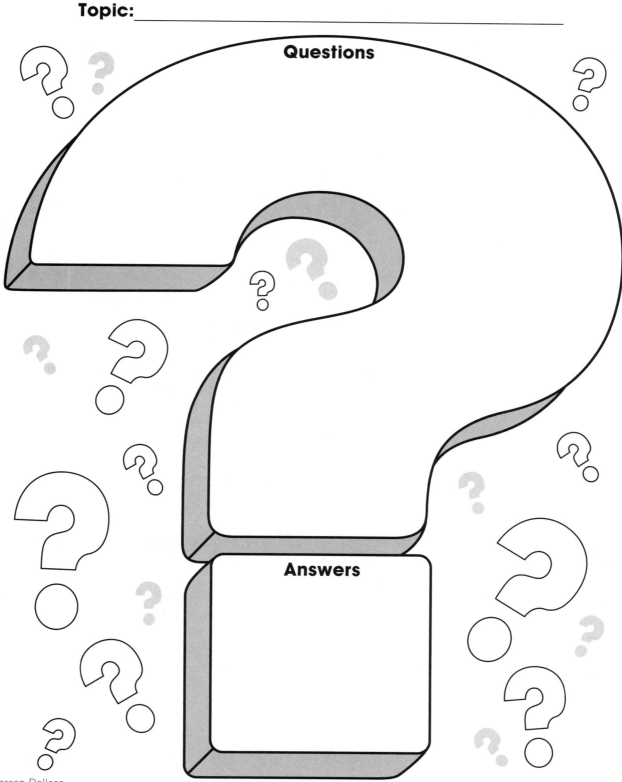

Questions

Answers

© Carson-Dellosa

Corralling a Cluster Map

Subject Area Uses

- All subject areas

Skills

- Classifying and categorizing
- Organizing information
- Comparing and contrasting information
- Connecting to prior knowledge

Purpose

Classifying information is a skill that requires higher-order thinking. Corralling a Cluster Map supports this skill by requiring students to generate and categorize key information. The organizer is designed for use during instruction or as an assessment tool once learning has taken place. The organizer is also useful for differentiation and is suitable for all ability levels and interests.

Using This Graphic Organizer

Corralling a Cluster Map provides students with a visual boundary for generating ideas about specific information. Model the use of the organizer by having students write topics in the barns and related information in the corrals.

The organizer is useful in many other ways:

- Reading: classifying and categorizing information about a character
- Writing: brainstorming ideas for an original piece on favorite foods or organizing information as it relates to a grammar rule
- Math: organizing information as it relates to a math rule or to show a fact family
- Science: classifying animals based on their characteristics or breed
- Social Studies: categorizing information on the types of homes American Indians live in based on their location
- Physical Education: recording information from comparing students' heart rates during specific exercises

Primary Model

This second-grade student used Corralling a Cluster Map as an assessment tool to show her understanding of how to classify nouns, verbs, adjectives, and adverbs. By using the organizer, the student could easily show her teacher her learning of parts of speech and organize information in a way that allowed her to see patterns within the organized lists.

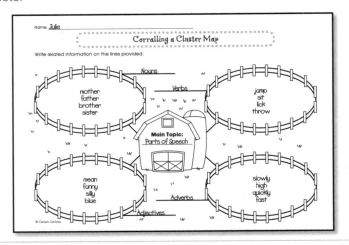

Intermediate Model

This third-grade student used Corralling a Cluster Map in math class to demonstrate her understanding of greatest common factors (GCFs) and least common multiples (LCMs). By using the organizer, the student was able to create a quick visual to show her teacher her understanding. She could also use it as a study guide for an upcoming quiz.

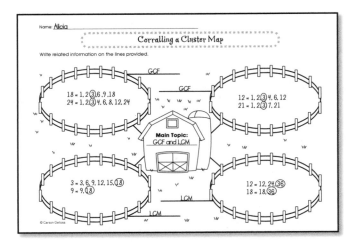

CD-104533 ■ © Carson-Dellosa

Corralling a Cluster Map

Write related information on the lines provided.

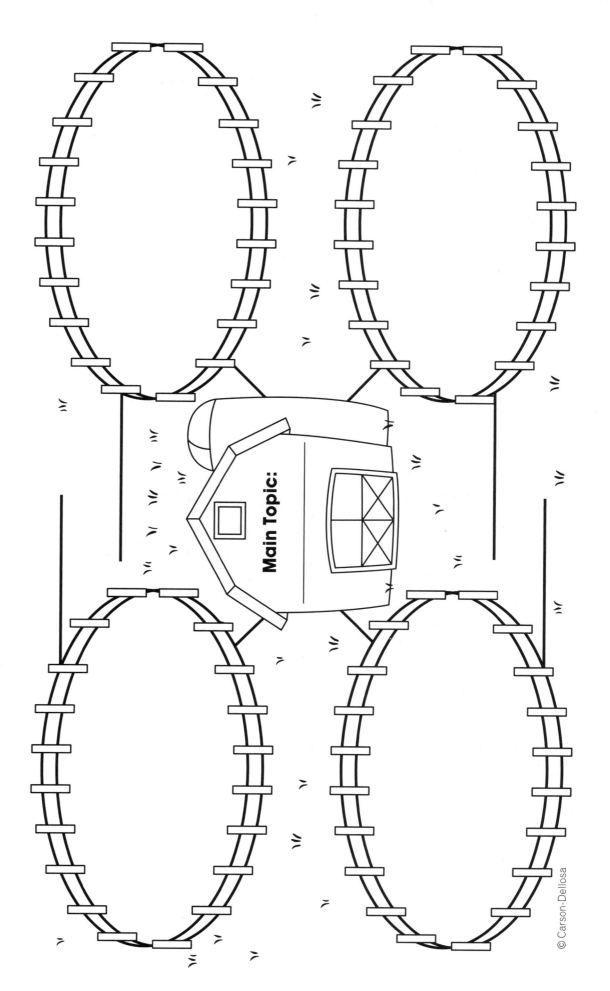

Main Topic:

© Carson-Dellosa

Climbing Through a Tree Map

Subject Area Uses
- Language Arts
- Science
- Social Studies
- Math
- Character Education

Skills
- Collecting and organizing information
- Sorting ideas
- Comparing and contrasting
- Drawing conclusions

Purpose
Climbing Through a Tree Map displays the hierarchy of a topic with its subparts. The organizer allows students to organize information for studying topics, brainstorming ideas, and planning written assignments. The organizer is also a tool that helps students learn to make connections between different ideas and details and is especially helpful when background knowledge is limited.

Using This Graphic Organizer
Model Climbing Through a Tree Map by placing a large copy on the board and having students choose topics to list in the tops of their trees. Have students list related information in each section thereafter to show relationships.

The organizer is useful in many other ways:

- Reading: comparing characters from a read-aloud story
- Writing: collecting and organizing information on parts of speech and providing examples of each
- Science: comparing and contrasting when experimenting on which baseball throw allows for the greater speed and distance
- Social Studies: comparing the roles of a mayor and a governor
- Math: describing steps for multiplication and division and providing examples of each or sorting shapes in a mini-unit on geometry
- Character Education: comparing reactions to situations that can make you angry or sad

Primary Model

This kindergarten student used Climbing Through a Tree Map in language arts class to show examples of the parts of speech. By using the organizer, the student was able to show the difference between nouns and verbs by including examples of each.

Intermediate Model

This fifth-grade student used Climbing Through a Tree Map during a small-group science experiment. The student collected data on the speed and distance of throwing a ball overhand and underhand. Using the organizer helped the student arrange the information to conclude that an overhand pitch moves faster and farther than an underhand pitch.

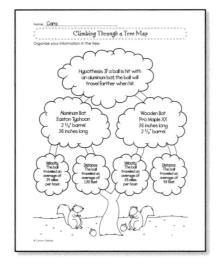

CD-104533 ■ © Carson-Dellosa

© Carson-Dellosa

Name: _____

Climbing Through a Tree Map

Organize your information in the tree.

Spinning a Web

Subject Area Uses
- Language Arts
- Science
- Social Studies
- Math

Skills
- Generating ideas
- Classifying information
- Making connections
- Comparing and contrasting

Purpose

For students to develop their writing skills, they must first learn to organize information. Spinning a Web is designed specifically to help students organize and analyze information. The organizer helps students develop writing skills for short stories and essays, read comprehensively, and make connections. The organizer is also a valuable tool that students may use in a variety of areas such as studying, generating ideas, and classifying thoughts. The organizer has many uses across the curriculum and is ideal for all ability levels.

Using This Graphic Organizer

Model the use of Spinning a Web by having students write topics in the centers of their diagrams. Have students fill in the supporting branches, or "legs," with ideas and the details supporting those ideas.

The organizer is useful in many other ways:

- Reading: comparing characters in a story by their characteristics
- Writing: generating thoughts and ideas for a new piece of writing
- Social Studies: generating ideas about how holidays are celebrated in different ways in different cultures
- Science: analyzing information that has been categorized to allow for future planning and constructing as students view the process of electricity and charges
- Math: comparing geometric figures by their attributes

Primary Model

This kindergarten student completed Spinning a Web after a unit on measurement. The teacher used the organizer to assess what the student had learned. By organizing the information, the student was able to clearly see the distinction between the two types of measurement described.

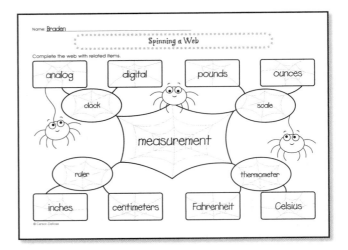

Intermediate Model

This fifth-grade student used Spinning a Web in science class as a summarizing tool to show the teacher what he learned from reading the assigned text. The student was able to use the space at the top to extend the web and expand the information to give the teacher a comprehensive look at the learning that took place.

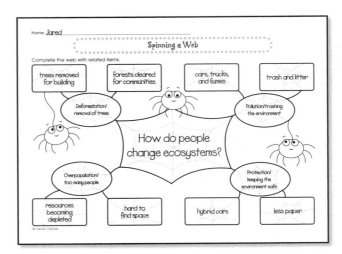

CD-104533 ■ © Carson-Dellosa

Name: _____

Complete the web with related items.

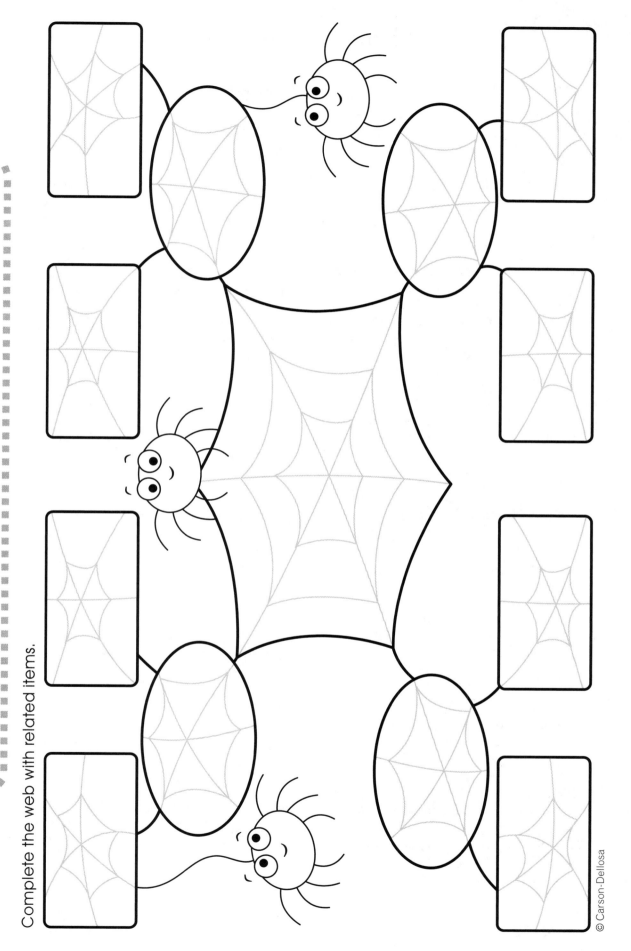

© Carson-Dellosa

A Penny for Your Thoughts

Subject Area Uses
- Language Arts
- Science
- Social Studies
- Math

Skills
- Using the think-pair-share strategy
- Analyzing and assessing information
- Comparing and contrasting
- Summarizing ideas
- Reflecting and formulating future thoughts

Purpose
A Penny for Your Thoughts is a think-pair-share active learning strategy that has many uses in virtually all subject areas. The organizer provides a dynamic way to get students to think and work cooperatively about reflective questions. By requiring students to use reflective questioning as opposed to a simpler recalling of facts, the organizer promotes higher-level thinking. The organizer is ideal for whole-class or small-group activities and is suited to students of all ability levels.

Using This Graphic Organizer
A Penny for Your Thoughts is designed to have students think through questions or topics in group situations. Have students list questions in the left column of the organizer. Then, have students answer the questions individually and record their thinking. As discussion follows, give students time to broaden or clarify their thinking before sharing.

The organizer is useful in many other ways:

- Reading: analyzing thoughts about characters within a selected text
- Math: analyzing and assessing information as students discuss making change with the fewest coins in a given situation
- Social Studies: comparing and contrasting different points of view during a debate about the importance of recycling
- Character Education: comparing student reactions about why it is important to follow specific classroom rules

This first-grade student used A Penny for Your Thoughts after a lesson on the difference between the day and night skies. By using the organizer, the student was able to share and compare his thoughts with another student before developing a common description of what they learned.

Intermediate Model

This fourth-grade student used A Penny for Your Thoughts with a classmate during math class to discuss probability. By using the organizer while working with partners, they were able to discuss what outcomes they felt would happen when flipping a coin. The organizer served as a record of their investigation.

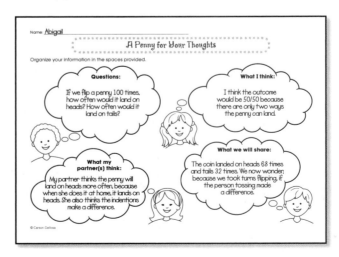

 CD-104533 ■ © Carson-Dellosa

Name: _____

A Penny for Your Thoughts

Organize your information in the spaces provided.

What I think:

What we will share:

Questions:

What my partner(s) think:

© Carson-Dellosa

Navigating Through Notes

Subject Area Uses
- Language Arts
- Science
- Social Studies
- Math

Skills
- Note taking
- Observing and recording information
- Analyzing and summarizing
- Predicting outcomes

Purpose
Being able to take notes and summarize information is important for any subject area and requires students to synthesize information. Navigating Through Notes is designed to help students organize information in a structured way. The organizer is useful in all subject areas, is ideal for students of any ability, and is extremely helpful to students who benefit from visually structured material.

Using This Graphic Organizer
Model using Navigating Through Notes by asking students to write their subjects or topics on the smaller notepaper. Then, have students use the larger notepaper to write concise notes that align with their topics.

The organizer is useful in many other ways:

- Reading: listing a series of events from a story read in guided reading or from a self-selected text
- Science: observing and recording the life cycle of a butterfly
- Social Studies: summarizing information about a famous person
- Math: organizing information learned about different tools used to measure objects

Primary Model

This second-grade student used Navigating Through Notes during a month-long observation on plant growth. By using the organizer, the student had a written record of his work. The organizer was helpful for when the teacher sent him to the classroom's science center.

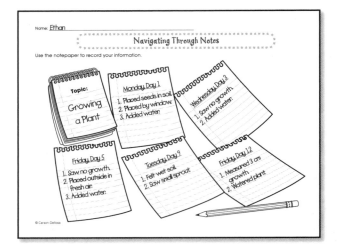

Intermediate Model

This fourth-grade student used Navigating Through Notes in social studies class to prepare an oral presentation on Johnny Appleseed. By using the organizer, the student was able to create a written record of her research and use it as a guide for preparing her speech.

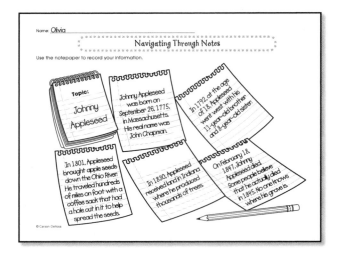

CD-104533 ■ © Carson-Dellosa

Name: _____

Navigating Through Notes

Use the notepaper to record your information.

Topic:

© Carson-Dellosa

Ready, Set, Research

Subject Area Uses
- Language Arts
- Science
- Social Studies

Skills
- Researching
- Organizing information
- Analyzing details
- Summarizing
- Using resources
- Developing questions

Purpose
The primary purpose for research is to discover and interpret information in a systematic way. Ready, Set, Research enables students to organize information in an easy-to-understand format. The organizer is a valuable tool for students to use when planning oral presentations, written reports, or projects.

Using This Graphic Organizer
Students will enjoy using Ready, Set, Research to organize their research topics and develop questions centered on their topics. Children are naturally curious and will enjoy using research tools to answer their own questions. Developing proper research skills will give them tools to answer any question. This organizer also provides space for students to record pertinent source information.

The organizer is useful in many other ways:

- Language Arts: using a variety of sources to obtain information for an oral report, a project, or a paper
- Science: researching facts about specific animals and their habitats
- Social Studies: researching information on historical figures

Primary Model

This first-grade student used Ready, Set, Research in science class during a guided lesson on birds using a nonfiction text entitled *Birds* by Susan Canizares and Pamela Chanko (Scholastic, 1998). During the lesson, the teacher showed the student how to find pertinent information from the shared text and organize it in the correct places in the organizer, making for easy review.

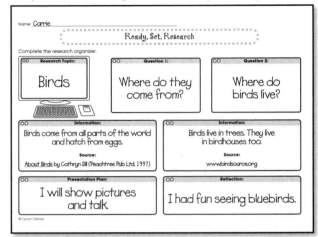

Intermediate Model

This fourth-grade student used Ready, Set, Research to complete an assignment on famous women for social studies class. The student researched information on Mary McLeod Bethune. By using the organizer, the student was able to summarize information about Bethune's life and understand her contributions in history. The organizer served as a data-collection tool for the student's written report.

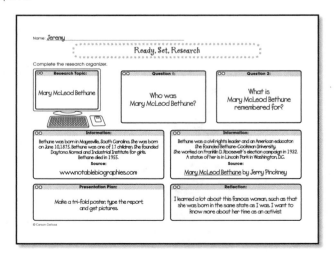

CD-104533 ■ © Carson-Dellosa

Name: _____

Ready, Set, Research

Complete the research organizer.

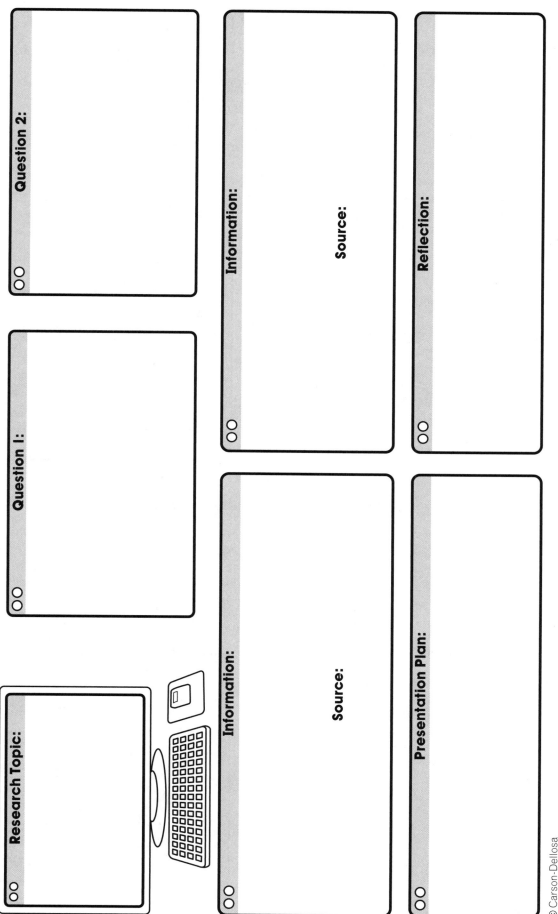

Research Topic:

Question 1:

Question 2:

Information:

Source:

Information:

Source:

Presentation Plan:

Reflection:

© Carson-Dellosa

Stirring Up Success

Subject Area Uses
- Science
- Social Studies
- Math

Skills
- Project planning
- Organizing information for research or projects
- Documenting information

Purpose
Being able to work cooperatively in a group setting is an important life skill. Stirring Up Success is a tool that allows students to practice social interaction while planning roles and responsibilities for a task. Perfect for use in small groups or partner settings, Stirring Up Success is multifunctional across the curriculum and is suited to differentiation with materials of varied levels.

Using This Graphic Organizer
Model the use of Stirring Up Success by walking students through the planning process provided on the organizer. Explain to students that they will need to decide as a group what tasks they will do and by whom. Have students continue to create plans for their projects and record their outcomes on their organizers.

The organizer is useful in many other ways:

- Science: investigating and planning a cooperative group experiment on the use of solar power or the importance of recycling
- Social Studies: planning roles and responsibilities for presentations about the Earth and the natural resources found there

Primary Model

A parent volunteer worked with a group of first-grade students using Stirring Up Success while creating and playing a math facts bingo game. By using the organizer, the students were able to determine their roles. The organizer also helped the students determine the importance of the activity, as well as provided them the opportunity to reflect on their work together.

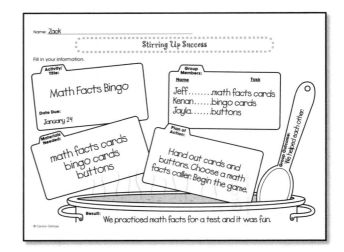

Intermediate Model

A group of third-grade students used Stirring Up Success to organize information while building a model of the solar system during science class. By using the organizer, each student was able to take an active role in the planning and the execution of the project. The organizer provided the teacher with a record to ensure that the students stayed on task.

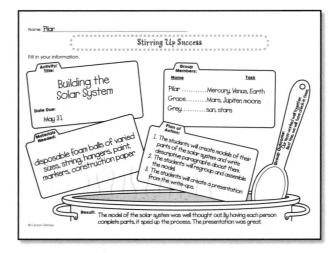

Name: _____

Stirring Up Success

Fill in your information.

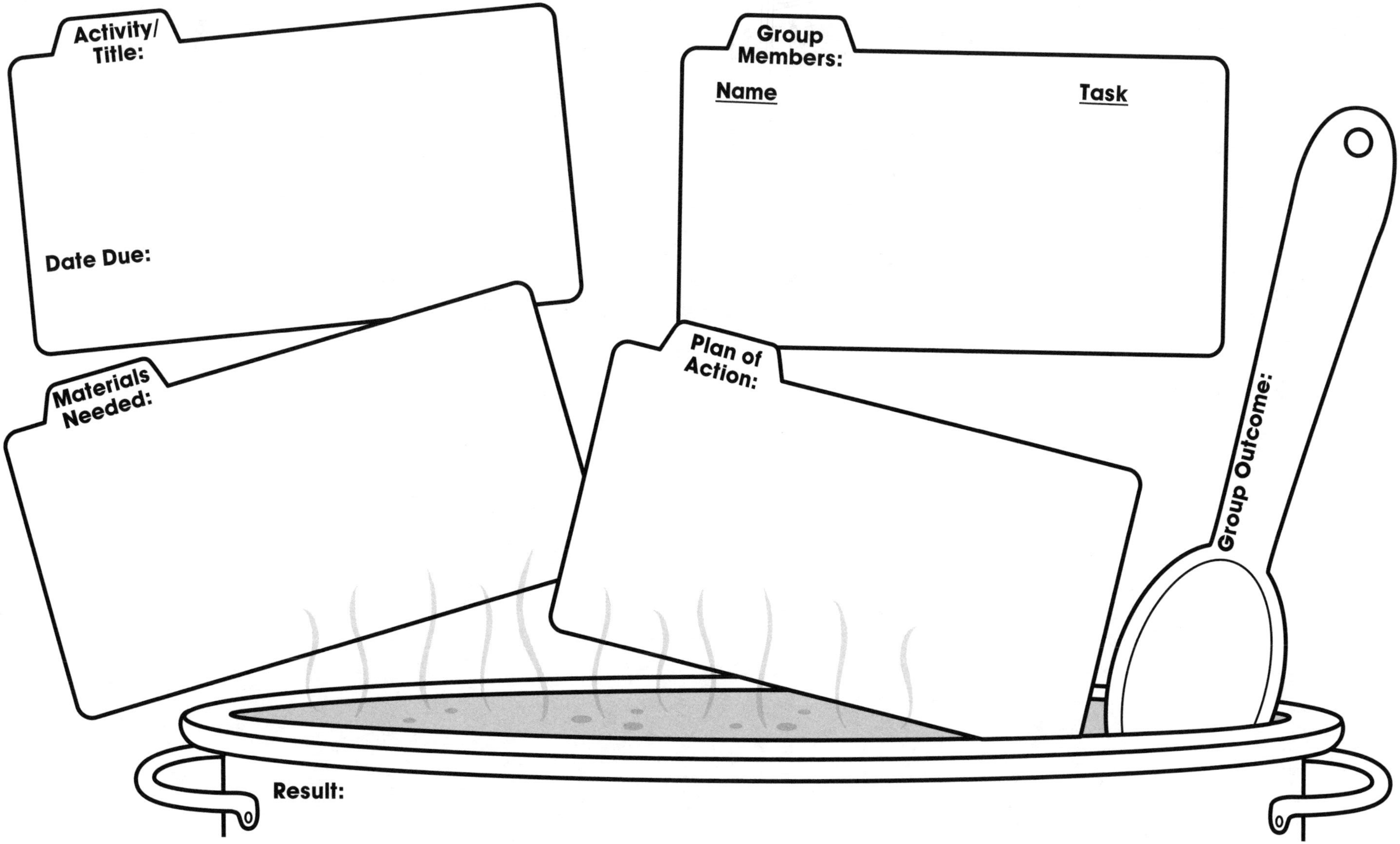

Group Outcome:

Group Members:

Task

Name

Plan of Action:

Activity/ Title:

Date Due:

Materials Needed:

Result:

© Carson-Dellosa

Engaging Experiments

Subject Area Uses
- Science
- Math

Skills
- Project planning
- Organizing information for research or projects
- Documenting information

Purpose
Hands-on science applications are essential in the early years and throughout school. Having students *actually do* science rather than just *learn* science is critical to growth in problem solving. Engaging Experiments is an organizer that enables students to use and record the process skills needed for carrying out experiments. The organizer is easy to use and is helpful in all grades and with students of varied ability levels.

Using This Graphic Organizer
Model the use of Engaging Experiments by walking students through the planning process provided on the organizer. Model how to form a hypothesis and record procedures and data in the appropriate areas on the organizer.

The organizer is useful in many other ways:

- Science: investigating and planning a cooperative group experiment on the use of solar power
- Math: investigating the probability of an outcome, such as how many red objects will be pulled from a bag of red, blue, and green objects after 100 draws

Primary Model

This second-grade student used Engaging Experiments during a unit on measurement. The student recorded the time it took for ice to melt using a Fahrenheit scale. By writing her information on the organizer, she had a visual record of her work that would help her explain her results to her teacher.

Intermediate Model

This fifth-grade student used Engaging Experiments to investigate how a wind generator could produce more energy. By using the organizer, the student was able to collect data, analyze data, and make conclusions about his experiment.

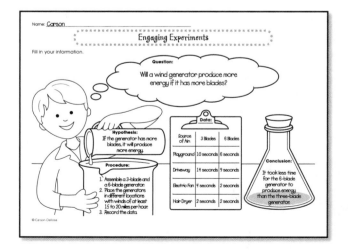

CD-104533 ■ © Carson-Dellosa

Name: _____

Engaging Experiments

Fill in your information.

Question:

Hypothesis:

Procedure:

Data:

Conclusion:

© Carson-Dellosa

A Spotted Survey

Subject Area Uses
- Math
- Science

Skills
- Completing surveys
- Collecting and organizing data
- Understanding tally marks
- Creating pictographs
- Understanding graphs

Purpose
Surveys are primary sources used for collecting information and making decisions. Students should have opportunities to give and take surveys early on, as it is a skill needed throughout their lives. A Spotted Survey enables students to collect and sort information as well as analyze data in many subject areas or settings. The organizer is ideal for working with students of all ability levels, whether as a remediation tool for an individual student, in a group project setting, or as a whole class.

Using This Graphic Organizer
A Spotted Survey helps students generate meaningful questions that they can ask their peers. Once students have collected the necessary information, they are able to compare the information and analyze it for meaning.

The organizer is useful in many other ways:

- Math: completing a survey with the use of tally marks to document the kinds of pets students have at home, to be followed up the next day with a class pictograph displaying the information
- Science: collecting and organizing data on each student's favorite season

Primary Model

This first-grade student used A Spotted Survey for data collection during a math lesson where students were asked to name their favorite fruits. In small groups, students took polls. By using the organizer, each student was able to create a written record of the collected data.

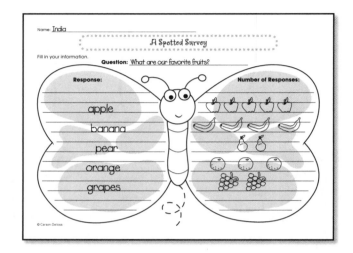

Intermediate Model

This student investigated the growth of a specific kind of plant while in science class. He surveyed the class to find out how many centimeters his peers thought the plant would grow over a two-week period. By using the organizer, the student was able to understand and analyze data for a follow-up graphing project in which he would graph the actual growth of the plant showing change over time.

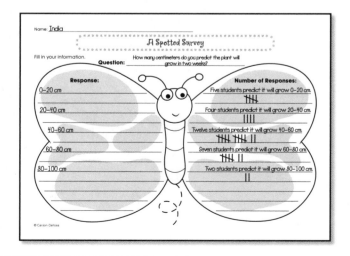

CD-104533 ■ © Carson-Dellosa

Name: _____

Fill in your information.

A Spotted Survey

Question: _____

Response:

Number of Responses:

© Carson-Dellosa

Diving into Data

Subject Area Uses
- Math
- Science

Skills
- Graphing (bar graphs, tally graphs, picture graphs, line plots)
- Organizing and comparing information
- Analyzing information for patterns

Purpose
Collecting, organizing, and analyzing data is important to teachers and students. Diving into Data is designed to allow students to organize data in a variety of situations. The organizer is a useful tool for students of any ability level and is suited to whole-group activities, small-group settings, and individual reteaching or enriching situations.

Using This Graphic Organizer
Diving into Data is ideal to model line plots, bar graphs, pictographs, and tally graphs. Graphs take many forms and are ideal for helping students organize information and make visual presentations. They are also useful aids for answering questions and solving problems.

The organizer is useful in many other ways:

- Math: graphing information by grade level from a recent school-wide service project such as collecting boxes of gifts for people serving in the military or creating bar graphs to represent test scores over a period of time
- Science: depicting data from an investigation by using a line plot to show growth of a plant or a grade level's favorite foods

Primary Model

This first-grade student used information on sorting shoes that was previously recorded during a math lesson where students took a survey. By using the organizer, the student was able to see a visual representation of the information collected and understand bar graphs and their relationships to surveys.

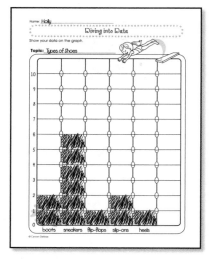

Intermediate Model

This fifth-grade student used previously recorded information from his science project on plant growth to graph the results on his Diving into Data organizer. By plotting the plant growth on the organizer, the student was able to determine the rate of growth and the plant's change over time. The organizer enabled the student to explore his work further to reflect on why the plant may or may not have grown more in one week than another.

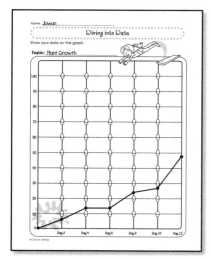

 CD-104533 ■ © Carson-Dellosa

Name: _____

Diving into Data

Show your data on the graph.

Topic: _____

© Carson-Dellosa

Sticky-Sweet Sorting

Subject Area Uses
- Language Arts
- Social Studies
- Science
- Math
- Character Education

Skills
- Comparing and contrasting with a two-circle Venn diagram
- Understanding similarities and differences
- Analyzing details
- Generalizing information

Purpose
Visual representations of similarities and differences are helpful in cementing concrete ideas. Sticky-Sweet Sorting is designed as a typical Venn diagram. It has two overlapping images that create a common area for identifying likenesses and outer areas for identifying differences. The organizer is a useful tool in many different subject areas and with students of all ability levels.

Using This Graphic Organizer
Model the use of Sticky-Sweet Sorting by placing a large copy on the board while comparing two items. Show students how to place information that is different in the outer areas to show contrast and information in the overlapping areas to show commonality.

The organizer is useful in many other ways:

- Reading: comparing and contrasting characters from a book read aloud in class or in a listening center
- Language Arts: serving as a prewriting tool for organizing thoughts before writing a compare-and-contrast essay
- Science: comparing similarities and differences of stars and planets
- Social Studies: comparing the job responsibilities of two community helpers
- Math: comparing and contrasting multiplication and division
- Character Education: listing similarities and differences between happy and sad feelings

Primary Model

This kindergarten student used Sticky-Sweet Sorting in a science center to compare rabbits and fish. The student was able to see a visual difference between the two types of animals. The organizer allowed the teacher to determine the student's ability to compare and contrast items.

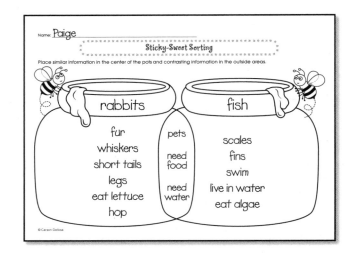

Intermediate Model

This fourth-grade student used Sticky-Sweet Sorting in PE class to compare his physical fitness at the beginning of the year to his fitness at the end of the year. By placing the information in the organizer, the student was able to see his improvement areas from August to June.

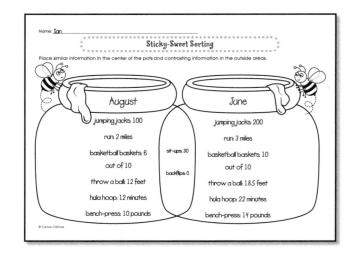

CD-104533 © Carson-Dellosa

Name: _____

Place similar information in the center of the pots and contrasting information in the outside areas.

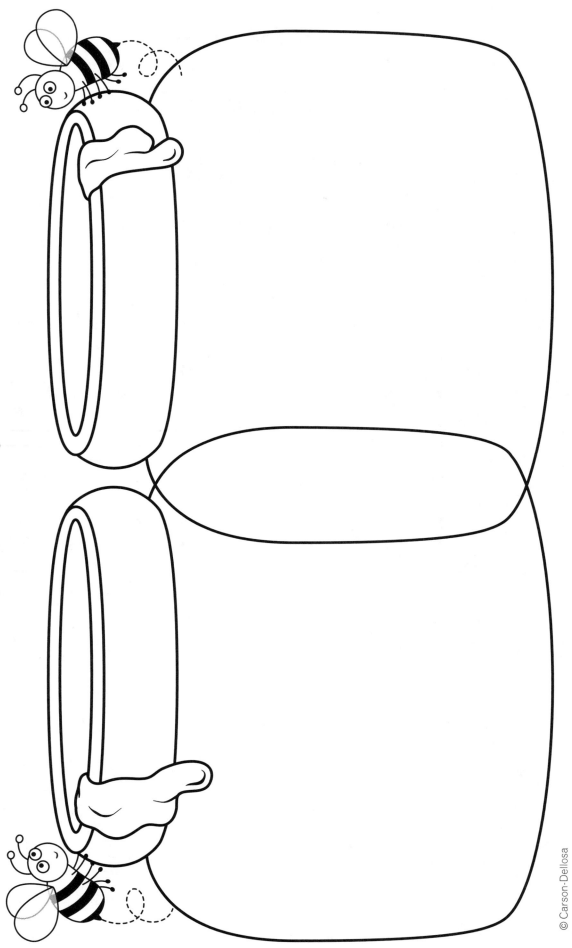

© Carson-Dellosa

A Sporty Sort

Subject Area Uses
- Language Arts
- Math
- Science
- Social Studies
- Character Education

Skills
- Comparing and contrasting with a three-circle Venn diagram
- Classifying and organizing information
- Illustrating similarities and differences
- Analyzing relationships

Purpose
A Venn diagram, normally made up of two or more circles, is used to visually organize information about concepts in a way that helps with recall and understanding of material. A Sporty Sort is useful in all subject areas and serves as both a teaching tool and an assessment to gauge learning. Usable in whole-group and small-group settings, A Sporty Sort is applicable to nearly any activity across the curriculum.

Using This Graphic Organizer
This graphic organizer is most useful in helping students to make their thinking visible. As a sorting tool, it visually displays all the elements of comparison. The teacher can model the use of A Sporty Sort across the curriculum and in a variety of formats.

The organizer is useful in many other ways:

- Reading: comparing and contrasting characters from text during guided reading
- Word Study: comparing word families or beginning sounds
- Social Studies: comparing currencies used around the world
- Science: comparing herbivores, omnivores, and carnivores
- Math: depicting similarities and differences of geometric shapes by their sides or angles
- Character Education: brainstorming alternative reactions to difficult situations such as walking away or ignoring

Primary Model

This first-grade student used A Sporty Sort during a science lesson to compare sea creatures. By using the organizer, the student could easily see the characteristics that made the creatures unique.

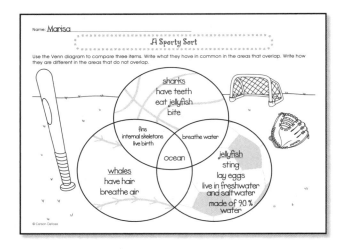

Intermediate Model

This fifth-grade student used A Sporty Sort in social studies class to compare and contrast the contributions of three historical figures. By using the organizer, the student was able to see what each had in common, as well as what made them so unique.

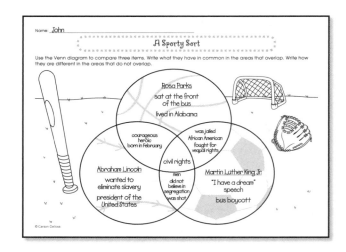

CD-104533 ■ © Carson-Dellosa

Name: _____

A Sporty Sort

Use the Venn diagram to compare three items. Write what they have in common in the areas that overlap. Write how they are different in the areas that do not overlap.

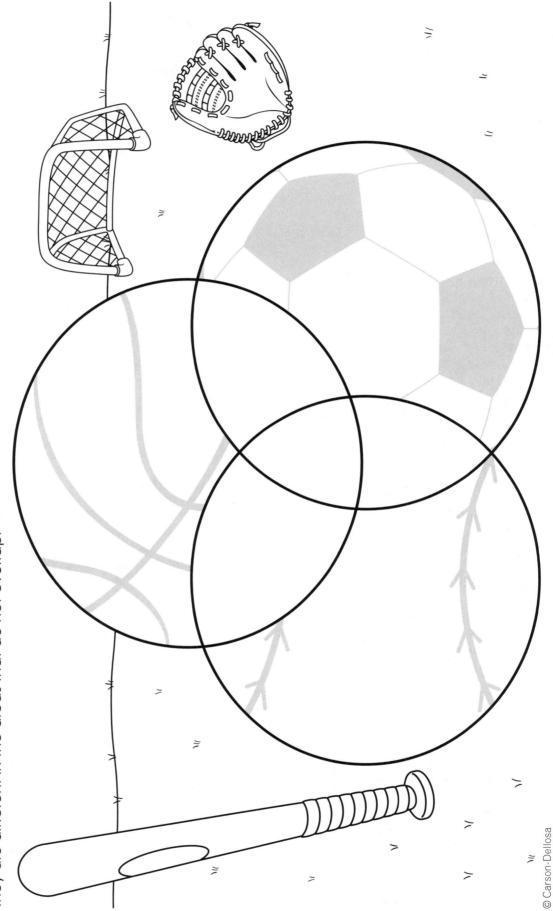

© Carson-Dellosa

Just Me as a T

Subject Area Uses
- Language Arts
- Science
- Social Studies
- Math
- Character Education

Skills
- Comparing and contrasting using a T-chart
- Organizing information
- Analyzing details

Purpose
Just Me as a T is a beneficial tool for students who are comparing or contrasting. The organizer works much in the same way as a Venn diagram without a middle group or a common area. Teaching students to compare and contrast enables them to think more critically and analytically. Just Me as a T helps students organize information in a coherent and visually appealing way so that they are better able to identify and understand similarities and differences.

Using This Graphic Organizer
Model the use of Just Me as a T during a whole-class activity by having students list attributes for one topic on the left and attributes for another topic on the right. Students may even personalize the organizers by filling in the faces of their characters or adding hair.

The organizer is useful in many other ways:

- Reading: comparing characters in a story read in a reading group
- Word Study: sorting words with different prefixes or suffixes
- Math: comparing and contrasting multiples of numbers to look for common factors
- Science: listing the differences between amphibians and reptiles
- Social Studies: comparing American Indians and colonists
- Character Education: comparing reactions to a disagreement during a discussion about being a good friend

Primary Model

This first-grade student used Just Me as a T during a math lesson to organize and analyze patterns in numbers when counting by 3s and 6s. By sorting the numbers, the student was able to see that 3 and 6 have numbers in common.

Intermediate Model

This fifth-grade student used Just Me as a T in science class after reading several informational texts on landforms and oceans. By organizing the information, the student was able to compare landforms and oceans and understand what makes them different from each other.

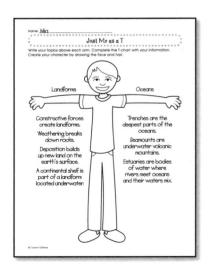

CD-104533 ■ © Carson-Dellosa

Name: _____

Write your topics above each arm. Complete the T-chart with your information.
Create your character by drawing the face and hair.

© Carson-Dellosa

One Sharp KWL

Subject Area Uses
- Language Arts
- Math
- Science
- Social Studies
- Character Education

Skills
- Activating prior knowledge
- Identifying a purpose for learning
- Recording and identifying information
- Classifying and organizing information

Purpose

Students bring beliefs and misconceptions to the classroom that can have a profound effect on their learning. The purpose of a KWL chart is to record prior knowledge, what students want to know, and what students learn after instruction. One Sharp KWL serves as a pre-assessment and provides opportunities to correct misinformation found during discussion of prior knowledge. Useful for setting a purpose for learning, the organizer also provides an excellent springboard for classroom conversation.

Using This Graphic Organizer

One Sharp KWL is a chart that consists of three columns. Model the use of the organizer by placing a large copy on the board and allowing students to list what they know about a topic in the first column, what they would like to know in the second column, and what they learned after instruction in the last column.

The organizer is useful in many other ways:

- Reading: discussing the details of an informational text read in class
- Word Study: recalling prior knowledge before a study on nouns or verbs
- Math: organizing information before, during, and after teaching a new unit on place value
- Science: classifying information before, during, and after a unit on magnets
- Social Studies: recording information learned during a unit on slavery
- Character Education: determining student misconceptions about bullying

Primary Model

This first-grade student used One Sharp KWL after a science lesson on sound. By organizing his thoughts, the student set a purpose for his learning and was better able to comprehend the material. The organizer also provided an assessment tool for the teacher to determine the progression of learning during the lesson.

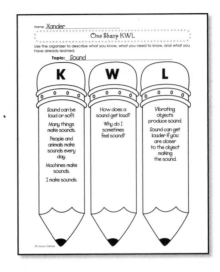

Intermediate Model

This fifth-grade student used One Sharp KWL in social studies class before, during, and after a mini-unit on the effects of immigration on the economy during the Industrial Revolution. By organizing her information, the student was able to focus her responses toward questions she had about the topic. The organizer also served as an assessment tool for the teacher so that he could identify what the student learned during the unit.

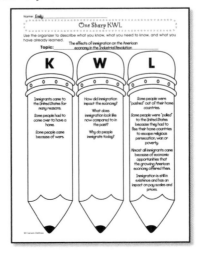

 CD-104533 ■ © Carson-Dellosa

Name: _____

One Sharp KWL

Use the organizer to describe what you know, what you need to know, and what you have already learned.

Topic:_____

K

W

L

© Carson-Dellosa

Subject Area Uses

- Language Arts
- Math
- Science

Skills

- Categorizing with a rule
- Organizing information
- Analyzing information
- Identifying similarities

Purpose

Classifying information based on a rule requires students to use higher-order thinking skills. One Rule for the Bunch is designed as a visual organizer to help students categorize information. By using the organizer to structure and arrange concepts or topics, students increase their ability to analyze information for similarities.

Using This Graphic Organizer

Model the use of One Rule for the Bunch by placing a large copy on the board. Have students place items in each grape that are alike based on a set of criteria.

The organizer is useful in many other ways:

- Reading: listing character traits from a text used in guided reading or reviewing for a test by using the organizer as a bingo board
- Word Study: identifying words with similar endings
- Math: identifying multiples of a number in math class
- Science: listing animals that are of the same species

Primary Model

This kindergarten student used One Rule for the Bunch during spelling to identify words that end with -ack. By using the organizer, she was able to see the spelling pattern and how the ending sound can be used to make new words.

Intermediate Model

This fifth-grade student used One Rule for the Bunch in math class as a homework assignment to show his knowledge of polygons. By using the organizer, the student was able to create a visual representation that would enable him to show his teacher what he had learned.

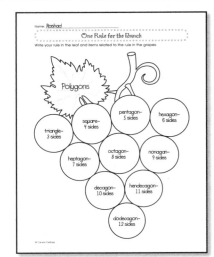

One Rule for the Bunch

Write your rule in the leaf and items related to the rule in the grapes.

© Carson-Dellosa

It's All in the Bag

Subject Area Uses
- Language Arts
- Math
- Science

Skills
- Sorting by attributes
- Classifying objects
- Reasoning
- Justifying
- Problem solving

Purpose
It's All in the Bag is a tool that enables students to sort objects by a rule or a set of rules. The organizer allows students to determine characteristics that objects do or do not have in common. By identifying how objects are alike and different, students practice reasoning, problem solving, and critical thinking. The organizer is ideal for small-group or whole-class activities and for differentiation because the user determines the rule. The sort can become more or less sophisticated, depending on the user.

Using This Graphic Organizer
Model the use of It's All in the Bag by having students place objects with similar characteristics in one bag and objects with differences in the other. Ask students to discuss the rules they chose for their sorting and/or list their criteria. You may also choose to supply the rules to differentiate the organizer based on ability levels.

The organizer is useful in many other ways:

- Word Study: identifying spelling words with specific patterns or sorting common and proper nouns in a language center
- Math: sorting polygons or coins by their characteristics or tools by what they measure
- Science: classifying animals by the number of legs they have

Primary Model
This kindergarten student used It's All in the Bag to sort buttons by their attributes during a math lesson. By using the organizer, the student was able to practice the higher-order activity of sorting, as well as justify her answers with a self-created rule.

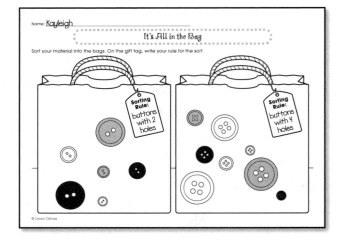

Intermediate Model
This fifth-grade student used It's All in the Bag in language arts class to sort idioms and examples of personification. By doing so, the student was able to distinguish between the two and provide a written record for his teacher of what he was learning.

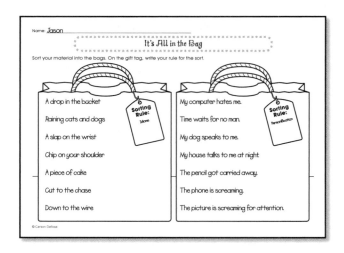

Name: _____

It's All in the Bag

Sort your material into the bags. On the gift tag, write your rule for the sort.

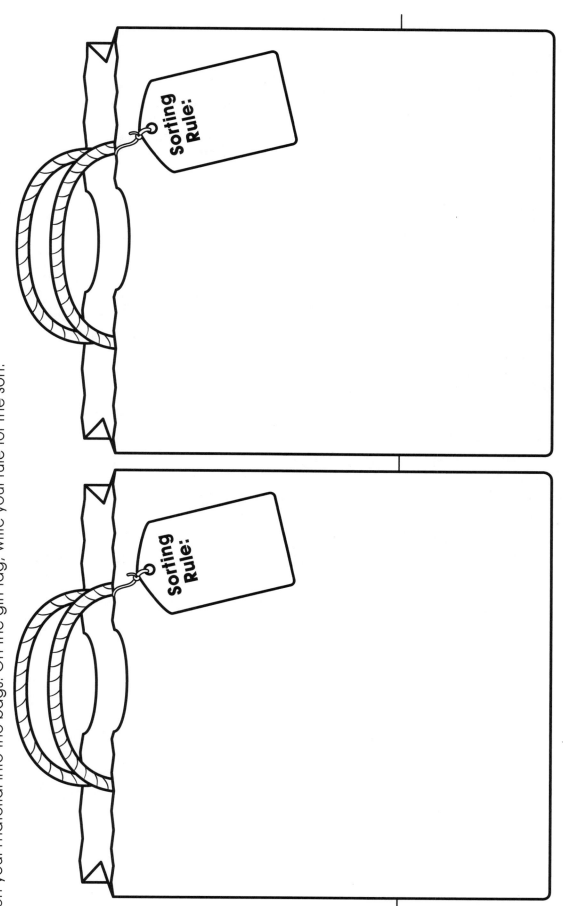

Sorting Rule:

Sorting Rule:

© Carson-Dellosa

Sign It with a Y

Subject Area Uses
- Language Arts
- Science
- Social Studies

Skills
- Analyzing information
- Organizing details
- Gathering information
- Making connections

Purpose
Y-charts allow students to record prior knowledge about a subject or a topic. Sign It with a Y is designed to help students think about topics and analyze details such as what something looks like, sounds like, or feels like. By thinking about topics while using their senses, students are able to make connections. Using their prior knowledge and beliefs, students can graphically display information in a way that aids in recall, connection, and comprehension. The organizer also allows for selection of what details students will analyze in each section.

Using This Graphic Organizer
Model the use of Sign It with a Y by asking students to select topics for discussion. Ask students to think critically about what the topics or the characters look like, sound like, or feel like (mood).

The organizer is useful in many other ways:

- Reading: describing the main character from a self-selected text or teacher read-aloud
- Science: describing animals in specific habitats during group work or peer investigation
- Social Studies: analyzing or describing what it would have been like to have lived during the time of slavery
- Character Education: describing what it means to share or to be kind to others

Primary Model

This kindergarten student used Sign It with a Y after a mini-unit on motion. After learning about how cars, planes, and buses move, the student watched a video about trains. He was then able to use the organizer to describe what he learned.

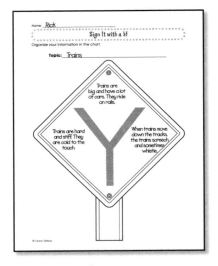

Intermediate Model

This fifth-grade student used Sign It with a Y in language arts class as a prewriting model before writing an essay on runaway slaves. By using the organizer, the student was able to organize important details that would add to the voice of her paper. By being required to think about how her character would look, feel, and sound, she included vivid language that her paper may not have had otherwise.

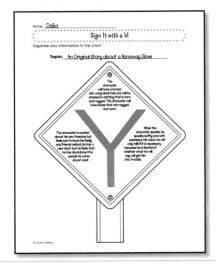

 CD-104533 ■ © Carson-Dellosa

Name: _____

Organize your information in the chart.

Topic: _____

© Carson-Dellosa

Weighing In on Fact and Opinion

Subject Area Uses
- Language Arts
- Social Studies
- Science

Skills
- Distinguishing between fact and opinion
- Analyzing details
- Comparing similarities and differences

Purpose
Identifying whether a statement expresses someone's opinion or contains facts that can be proven is a critical skill for listening, speaking, reading, and writing. Many students do not understand the difference between a statement of fact that can be proven and a statement of opinion, which is someone's belief or feeling. Weighing In on Fact and Opinion is an organizer designed to create a visual picture that helps students skillfully make decisions based on evidence. The organizer is a useful tool to use before, during, or after instruction and is ideal in whole-group, small-group, or individual settings.

Using This Graphic Organizer
As students begin to use Weighing In on Fact and Opinion, have them list all of the facts they know on a particular subject or topic on the left sides of their organizers. Have them write information they determine to be opinions on the right sides. Once completed, have students extend their learning by making decisions about their topics.

The organizer is useful in many other ways:

- Reading: listing facts and opinions about a character or characters in a text
- Science: identifying what a student believes to be factual or untrue about an animal or an insect they learning about
- Social Studies: organizing information about a presidential candidate based on Internet research or creating a study guide for an upcoming debate

Primary Model

This first-grade student used Weighing In on Fact and Opinion during a reading lesson. After a mini-lesson on wolves, the teacher asked the student to glue facts or opinions in the correct sections on sentence strips. By using the organizer, the student was able to understand that opinion statements contain clue words or feeling words.

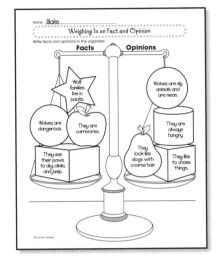

Intermediate Model

This third-grade student used Weighing In on Fact and Opinion in science class during a mini-unit on the seasons. The student learned about misconceptions and truths about the seasons. The organizer allowed the student to understand that while people have specific beliefs about each of the four seasons, only statements that can be proven are actual facts.

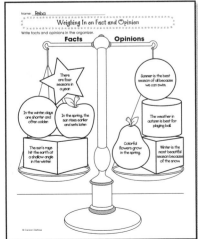

CD-104533 ■ © Carson-Dellosa

Name: _____

Weighing In on Fact and Opinion

Write facts and opinions in the organizer.

Facts   **Opinions**

© Carson-Dellosa

Pros or Cons

Subject Area Uses
- Language Arts
- Science
- Social Studies
- Character Education

Skills
- Comparing pros and cons
- Weighing decisions
- Organizing information

Purpose

Decision making is a skill that all students need to help them deal with situations they will encounter throughout their lives. Pros or Cons enables students to list and analyze two different sides of a topic or an issue. By weighing opposing sides of an argument effectively, students are better equipped to make decisions. The organizer is applicable in any subject area and even as an everyday tool for making personal decisions.

Using This Graphic Organizer

Pros or Cons challenges students to organize information into categories based on their knowledge of a topic. After presenting both sides, model with students how to make a deliberate decision.

The organizer is useful in many other ways:

- Reading: evaluating a character's decision in a story read aloud
- Science: making an argument for or against living green and whether it is best for the environment
- Social Studies: debating about who should be president, mayor, or chief of police
- Character Education: weighing decisions about studying daily rather than the night before a test along with a family member, a teacher, or a parent volunteer

Primary Model

This first-grade student used Pros or Cons for a language arts homework assignment. While working with a family member to evaluate how important it is to complete homework daily, the student was able to make an informed decision on why it would benefit him to be consistent.

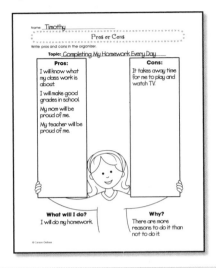

Intermediate Model

This fifth-grade student used Pros or Cons during social studies class to weigh the decision to vote. By using the organizer, the student was able to better understand the voting process and evaluate whether she thought that it was an important thing for a citizen to do.

CD-104533 ■ © Carson-Dellosa

Name: _____

Write pros and cons in the organizer.

Topic: _____

Pros:

Cons:

What will I do?

Why?

© Carson-Dellosa

Raining Cause and Effect

Subject Area Uses
- Language Arts
- Science
- Social Studies

Skills
- Understanding cause and effect
- Analyzing relationships found within texts
- Examining the causes and the consequences of events and ideas

Purpose
Raining Cause and Effect allows both primary and intermediate students to analyze how different actions result in different effects. Understanding cause and effect is an important life skill. The organizer enables primary students to tell what and why things happen. Intermediate students are able to investigate further by evaluating an outcome to determine how a different set of actions can lead to different results. This practical tool also offers a way of assessing learning.

Using This Graphic Organizer
Model the use of Raining Cause and Effect by placing a large copy on the board. Demonstrate causal relationships by setting up a row of dominoes on a table, pushing one of the dominoes down, and then discussing what happened. Then, ask students to write examples of cause-and-effect sentences appropriately in the clouds and the puddles.

The organizer is useful in many other ways:

- Language Arts: analyzing story elements and how the effect can be altered if the cause is changed
- Social Studies: looking at connections between the events leading up to the Battle of Cowpens
- Science: examining the outcomes of plants that are taken care of differently (for example, one with more sunlight than the other)

Primary Model

This first-grade student investigated weather with Raining Cause and Effect. By using the organizer, the student was able to see clear connections between each cause and the related effect. The organizer was a visual record for the teacher to gauge learning.

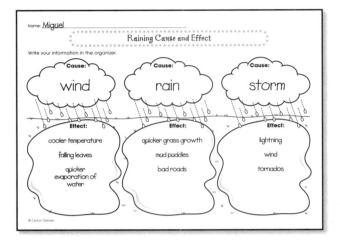

Intermediate Model

This fifth-grade student used Raining Cause and Effect during science class to investigate the causal relationships of high and low tides. After completing an Internet search on the impacts of each, the student was able to make connections about what happens during each tidal phase.

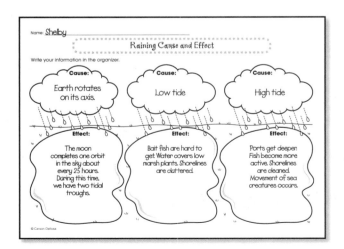

Name: _____

Raining Cause and Effect

Write your information in the organizer.

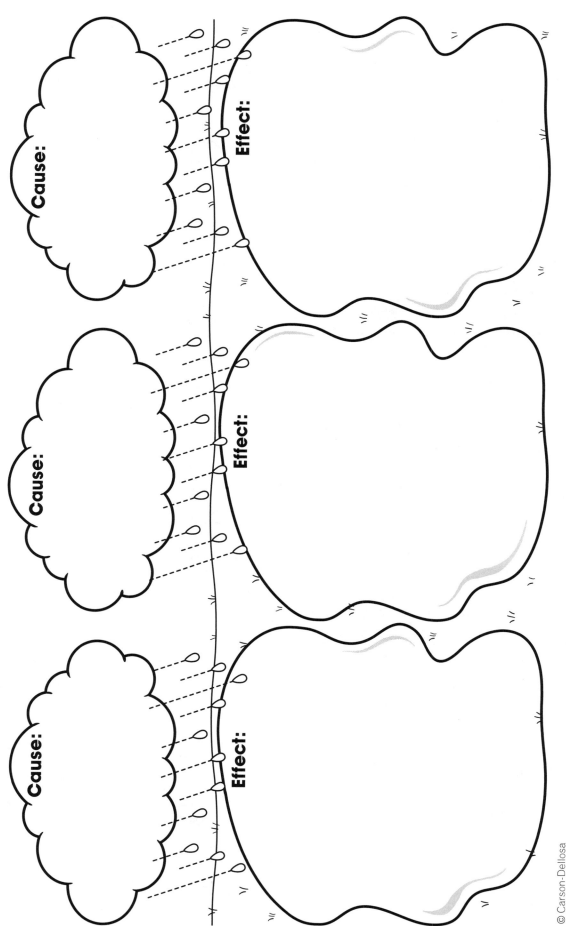

Cause:

Cause:

Cause:

Effect:

Effect:

Effect:

© Carson-Dellosa

Something Is a Little Fishy

Subject Area Uses
- Language Arts
- Science
- Social Studies

Skills
- Analyzing cause and effect
- Organizing information
- Mapping
- Identifying end results

Purpose
Fish-bone organizers are ideal for showing causal relationships. Something Is a Little Fishy is designed to help students build reading comprehension and prewriting skills by organizing main ideas and supporting details. The use of a fish-bone mapping organizer allows students to challenge a previously thought concept, analyze the information, and construct a plan to change the effect. The organizer is ideal for building natural interest and curiosity, which in turn encourages students to generate alternatives or solve problems.

Using This Graphic Organizer
With Something Is a Little Fishy, have students begin by listing their effects on the centers of their fish. Have students analyze the causes and write them on the horizontal lines. Then, have students add details that correspond to the contributing causes on the lines stemming from the horizontal lines.

The organizer in useful in many other ways:

- Reading: analyzing in a whole-group discussion the outcome of a story based on events leading up to it
- Science: identifying the causes and effects of air pollutants
- Social Studies: describing the effects of not following directions on a map

Primary Model

This second-grade student used Something Is a Little Fishy after a field trip to the zoo. The student identified what made the trip a success. By using the organizer, he was able to see the relationship between how good weather, students with good character, interesting animals, and nice teachers made the trip so much fun.

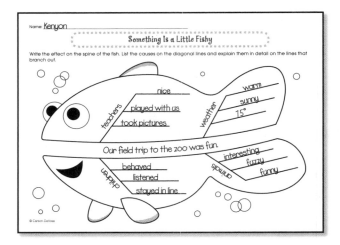

Intermediate Model

This fifth-grade student used Something Is a Little Fishy in science class to identify four types of water pollutants and what causes them. By using the organizer, the student was able to understand the causes of the large overall problem of pollution. She then extended her learning to write a story about a make-believe fish that must survive in these types of polluted areas.

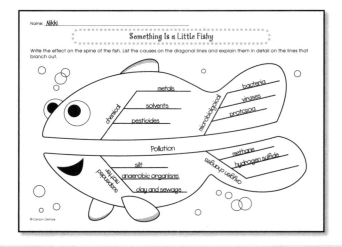

CD-104533 ■ © Carson-Dellosa

Name: _____

Something Is a Little Fishy

Write the effect on the spine of the fish. List the causes on the diagonal lines and explain them in detail on the lines that branch out.

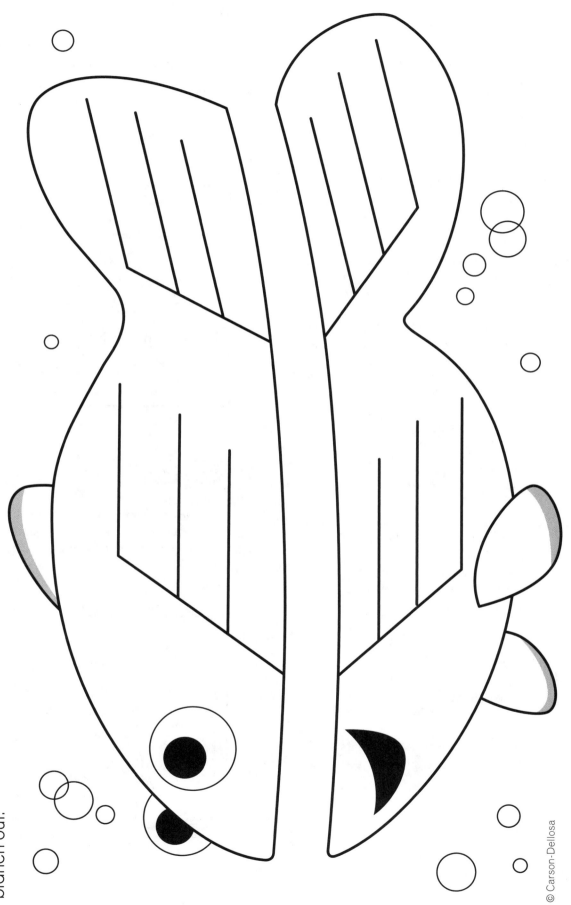

© Carson-Dellosa

A Colorful Matrix

Subject Area Uses
- Language Arts
- Social Studies
- Science

Skills
- Classifying and comparing using a matrix
- Sorting and analyzing details
- Organizing information

Purpose

A Colorful Matrix helps students organize and compare characteristics. It is an effective visual aid that displays a simple structure. The organizer enables students to list features of an item and simplify the process of analysis. Students are then able make in-depth comparisons of multiple objects and their characteristics all at once. The organizer is an ideal tool for use in all subject areas, particularly in science and reading, and is appropriate for students of all ability levels.

Using This Graphic Organizer

As students begin to use A Colorful Matrix, it is important that they understand they are listing the items to be compared on the left side of the page and the characteristics to be compared across the top. Model the use of the organizer by placing a large copy on the board and listing several characters from a read-aloud on the organizer.

The organizer is also useful in many other ways:

- Reading: comparing characteristics of main characters and supporting characters in text
- Social Studies: identifying characteristics of cities within a state such as population
- Science: sorting and identifying characteristics of several plants such as height, color, and sunlight needs

Primary Model

This second-grade student used A Colorful Matrix during a science lesson to classify information about animal habitats. The organizer allowed the student to instantly see similarities and differences among animals she is familiar with.

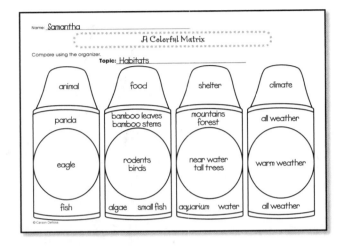

Intermediate Model

This fifth-grade student used A Colorful Matrix during social studies to identify areas around the world. By using the organizer at the computer station, the student learned specific information about the areas, as well as their distinguishable symbols, and was able to record the information in a visually organized format.

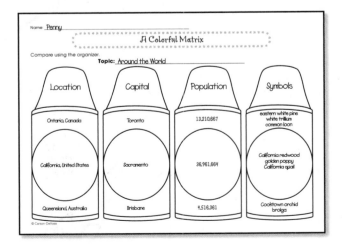

Name: _____

A Colorful Matrix

Compare using the organizer.

Topic: _____

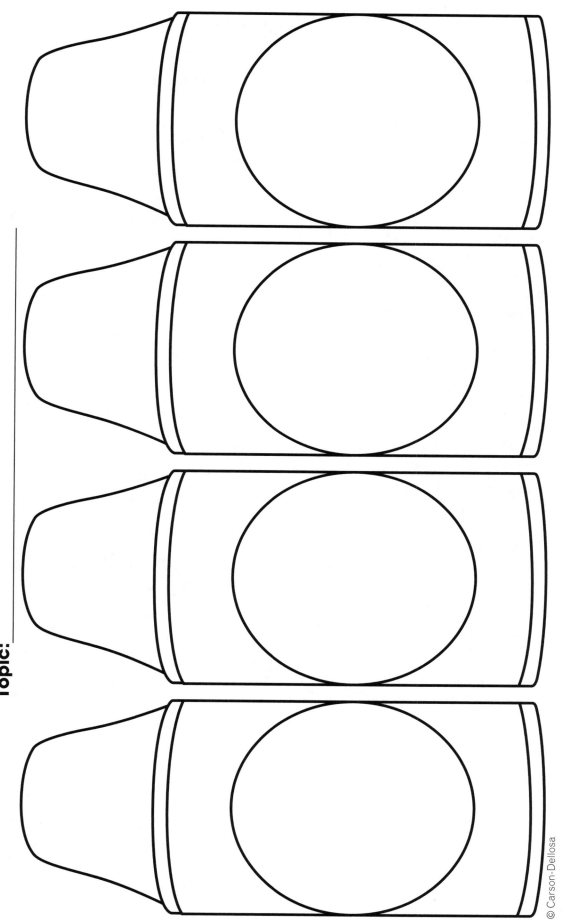

© Carson-Dellosa

A Magnificent Map

Subject Area Uses
- Social Studies
- Math

Skills
- Mapping
- Organizing information
- Understanding and explaining information

Purpose
Understanding geography and how it impacts people's lives based on where they live is essential to the study of social studies. One of the best ways for a student to understand spatial forms and the relationships between geography and people's lives is to actively participate in creating maps. With A Magnificent Map, students are able to place themselves in relationship to their classes, schools, communities, or homes and develop a greater interest in, as well as a true understanding of, the benefits of maps.

Using This Graphic Organizer
Model the use of A Magnificent Map by placing a large copy on the board and having students help draw a map of the classroom.

The organizer is useful in many other ways:

- Social Studies: showing a neighborhood, a community, or a map of an area studied from a time period in history; assessing student learning of using a key, directional words, etc.; designing or drawing a scale map of the school playground
- Math: outlining the steps to solving a word problem

Primary Model
This first-grade student used A Magnificent Map to show where things were located in his classroom. By using the organizer, the student was better able to use positional words and describe his surroundings.

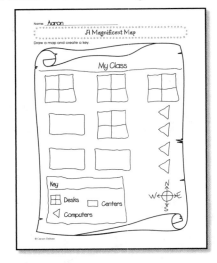

Intermediate Model
This fifth-grade student used A Magnificent Map in social studies class as an assessment to record information from a research project on major earthquakes recorded around the world. By using the organizer, the student was able to provide a visual record of her learning.

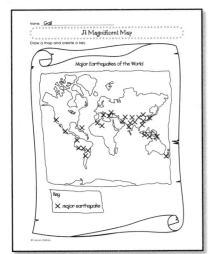

Name: _____

A Magnificent Map

Draw a map and create a key.

© Carson-Dellosa

Subject Area Uses

- Language Arts
- Science
- Social Studies
- Character Education

Skills

- Evaluating
- Making decisions based on information or data
- Reflecting and formulating future thoughts

Purpose

I Spy a PMI Chart is an organizer with very distinct features. PMI stands for Pluses, Minuses, and Interesting Implications. The purpose of the organizer is to increase a student's ability to distinguish between positive and negative issues pertaining to a topic and the ability to make decisions. The organizer is ideal in concept areas such as science or social studies and easily fits into the curriculum with students of all ability levels.

Using This Graphic Organizer

Model the use of I Spy a PMI Chart by placing a large copy on the board. Have students write positive elements of an issue in the P (Pluses) column, negative elements in the M (Minuses) column, and interesting information that relates to the material in the I (Interesting Implications) column.

The organizer is useful in many other ways:

- Language Arts: analyzing a character in a selected text during a whole-group discussion
- Social Studies: examining why people moved westward
- Science: evaluating a specific animal in science to determine whether the animal is more of a benefit or a risk
- Character Education: weighing the benefits of following rules

Primary Model

This second-grade student used I Spy a PMI Chart to assess her map project. The organizer enabled the student to evaluate her plan for the project, think about how she might have improved her work, and list what she learned throughout the process.

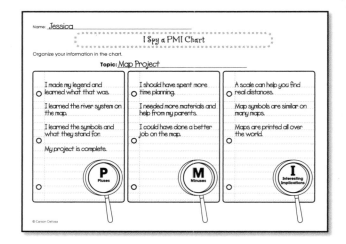

Intermediate Model

This fourth-grade student used I Spy a PMI Chart while researching information for a science project in which he would investigate the positives and negatives for keeping snakes as pets. By using the chart, the student was able to develop a clear thesis for his project.

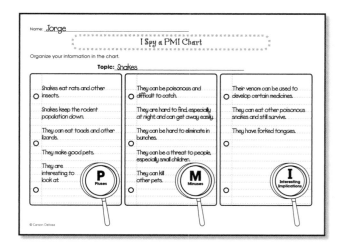

Name: _____

I Spy a PMI Chart

Organize your information in the chart.

Topic: _____

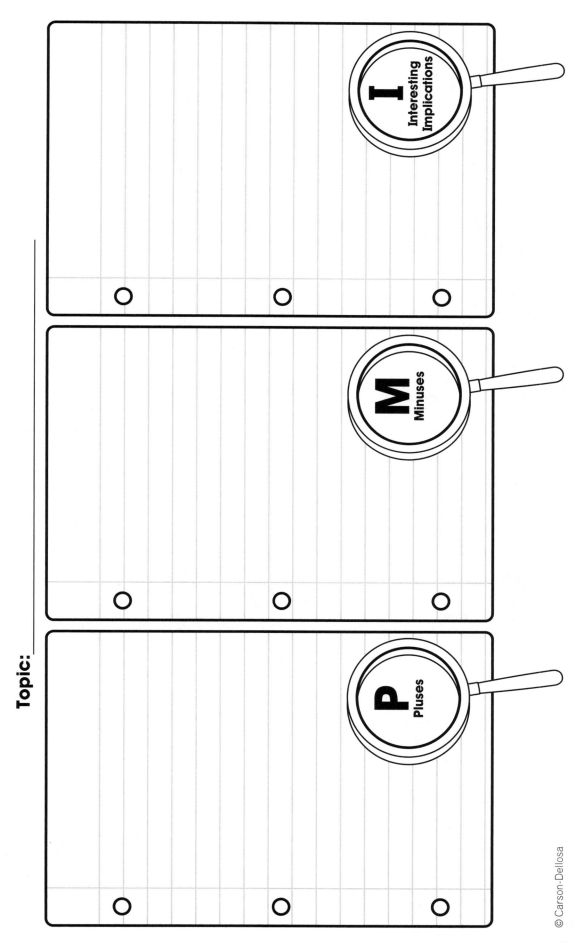

I — Interesting Implications

M — Minuses

P — Pluses

© Carson-Dellosa

A Window into Words

Subject Area Uses
- Language Arts
- Social Studies
- Science
- Math

Skills
- Developing vocabulary
- Illustrating terms
- Writing with meaning
- Comparing and contrasting
- Decoding words

Purpose
Understanding vocabulary is critical to reading comprehension. Organizers that require students to define and visualize words are useful tools that help with comprehension. A Window into Words is designed to help students represent vocabulary with definitions, examples and non-examples (antonyms), sentences, and drawings. This in-depth look into words helps provide a solid foundation that supports comprehension of read or learned material. The organizer is useful for vocabulary instruction as well as independent student work. By providing a quick look at students' vocabulary knowledge, the organizer also serves as a learning assessment tool.

Using This Graphic Organizer
Have students use A Window into Words to identify vocabulary terms, their definitions, and their synonyms and antonyms. Then, have students use the organizer to write sentences and draw pictures that represent the words.

The organizer is useful in many other ways:

- Reading: defining vocabulary words from selected text to enrich meaning and comprehension
- Science: illustrating terms during a weather unit
- Math: defining terms in geometry such as lines, rays, and line segments
- Social Studies: defining key terms in a unit on the forming of the United States

Primary Model

This second-grade student used A Window into Words during a science unit to organize and record the meaning of words learned during a unit study on clouds. The organizer enabled the student to understand the words at a deeper level by allowing him to visualize and see examples and non-examples (antonyms) of the words.

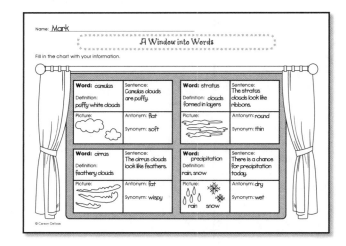

Intermediate Model

This fifth-grade student used A Window into Words in math class during a unit on geometry. By defining and drawing each geometric term, the student had a better understanding of the words, their meanings, and their use.

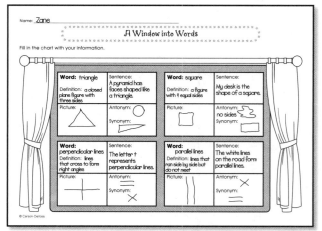

CD-104533 ■ © Carson-Dellosa

Name: _____

A Window into Words

Fill in the chart with your information.

Word:	Sentence:	Word:	Sentence:
Definition:		Definition:	
Picture:	Antonym:	Picture:	Antonym:
	Synonym:		Synonym:

Word:	Sentence:	Word:	Sentence:
Definition:		Definition:	
Picture:	Antonym:	Picture:	Antonym:
	Synonym:		Synonym:

© Carson-Dellosa

Pedaling Through a Problem

Subject Area Uses
- Math
- Science

Skills
- Problem solving
- Organizing information
- Making predictions

Purpose

Having a clear and concise set of steps to solve a problem can be helpful in all areas of the curriculum. Pedaling Through a Problem enables students to move through a series of steps to solve a problem. This is especially helpful to be able to assess where intervention is needed. By using the organizer, students have a structure to guide them toward a solution, ensuring that nothing is overlooked.

Using This Graphic Organizer

Model the use of Pedaling Through a Problem by having students write their problems in the small wheels at the back of the figures. Have students complete each step in the larger wheel to come to a solution. Then, have students check their work for accuracy.

The organizer is useful in many other ways:

- Math: solving word problems individually or in small groups or differentiating instruction for a student who is having difficulty solving problems such as addition and subtraction with regrouping
- Science: making predictions and solving problems during a science experiment
- Character Education: enabling students to solve an issue where a negative reaction has occurred in a character education class

Primary Model

This first-grade student used Pedaling Through a Problem in math class to dissect a word problem. By using the organizer, the student was able to find useful information for solving the problem and eliminate unnecessary information. The organizer helped the teacher see that the student had a clear understanding of how to solve an addition word problem.

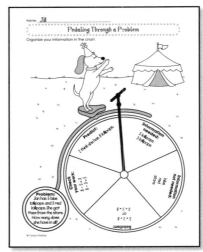

Intermediate Model

This fifth-grade student used Pedaling Through a Problem in science class to investigate how surface affects the movement of objects. By using the organizer, the student learned how to set up a science project and predict its outcome. The student also discovered that friction creates lag. The organizer enabled the teacher to see that the student understood each part of a scientific process.

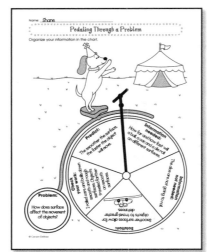

CD-104533 ■ © Carson-Dellosa

Name: _____

Pedaling Through a Problem

Organize your information in the chart.

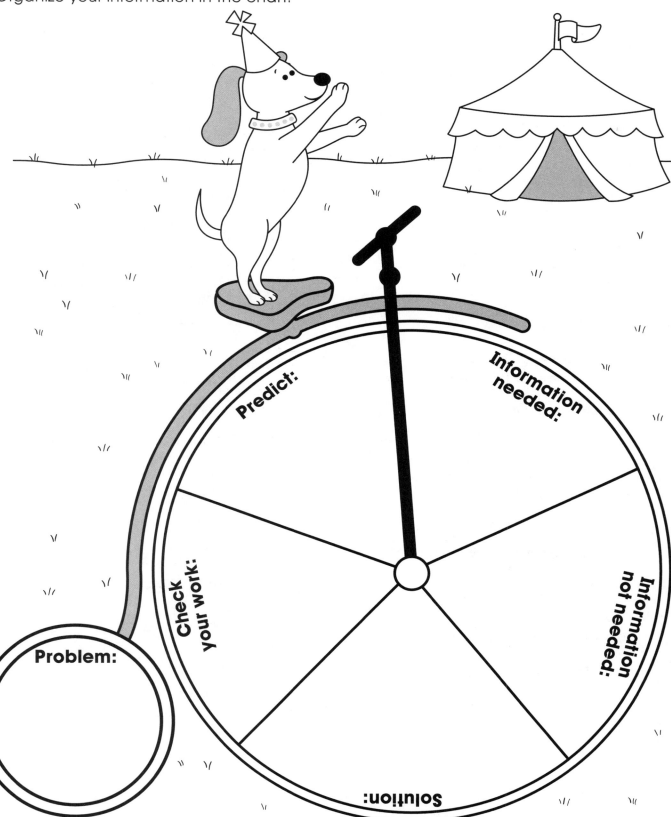

Predict:

Information needed:

Check your work:

Information not needed:

Problem:

Solution:

© Carson-Dellosa

Subject Area Uses

- All subject areas

Skills

- Summarizing and reflecting
- Organizing and assessing

Purpose

Using exit slips to informally assess students is an effective way to differentiate instruction. This form of evaluation helps with identifying students' understanding of new or old information. Exit This Way is designed to stimulate critical thinking and provide insight into student learning. The organizer is useful across the curriculum and is ideal to use with students of all ability levels.

Using This Graphic Organizer

Exit slips provide a way for students to write and provide information about what they think about the class, a topic under discussion, or a specific teaching strategy. Have students use Exit This Way organizers at the end of class and turn them in for assessment. This is a useful teacher tool for assessing where more instruction may be necessary.

The organizer is useful in many other ways:

- Reading: assessing whether students understood the elements of a story
- Word Work: gauging understanding of grammar rules
- Science: summarizing and reflecting on a lesson on magnetism in science
- Social Studies: using as a quiz after a lesson on the development of the U.S. Constitution

Primary Model

This first-grade student used Exit This Way with a parent volunteer after a lesson on shapes. By using the organizer, the student was able to record what he learned and connect it to the world around him.

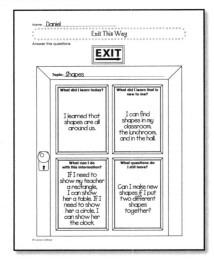

Intermediate Model

This fourth-grade student used Exit This Way after a science lesson on magnetism. The student learned that magnets have north and south poles and that they only stick to opposite sides. The organizer then served as a tool for the teacher to assess the student's learning.

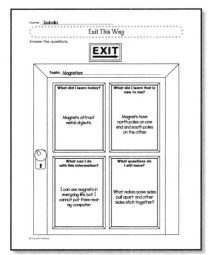

CD-104533 ■ © Carson-Dellosa

Name: _____

Answer the questions.

Topic: _____

What did I learn today?

What did I learn that is new to me?

What can I do with this information?

What questions do I still have?

© Carson-Dellosa

Subject Area Uses

- All subject areas

Skills

- Organizing and reviewing information
- Sequencing information

Purpose

Providing students with a visually structured way to study information or complete written assignments is important across the curriculum to help support recall and understanding. All Boxed In is designed to help students organize their work into small sections for review and study. By using the organizer, students gain the ability to remember information more quickly, as well as comprehend the material.

Using This Graphic Organizer

Model the use of All Boxed In by placing information that is related across one row or down one column. This graphic organizer is a helpful visual that highlights the parts of a whole, the details of a theme, or the examples of a specific idea.

The organizer is useful in many other ways:

- As an error-analysis sheet for students to rework problems on an assessment in any subject area
- As an organized sheet for working math problems
- As a study guide for listing information for an upcoming test
- As a storyboard for a writing assignment or to help recall a story read in a guided reading lesson
- For practicing vocabulary as students use the boxes to list words, definitions, synonyms, and picture representations
- As a word wall list for the month
- As a record for spelling words of the week

Primary Model

This first-grade student used All Boxed In to create a tool to help him study punctuation. By using the organizer, the student was able to create an organized way to review, which in turn helped him with recall.

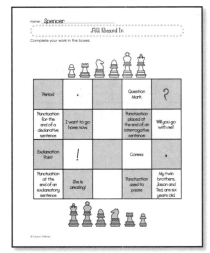

Intermediate Model

This fifth-grade student used All Boxed In as a record of error analysis. The student reworked missed items from a benchmark test in math in the boxes on the organizer. By using the organizer, the student was able to identify and correct his own errors. The organizer also served as a record for the teacher to use to see if the problems originally missed on the benchmark were simple mistakes or a misunderstanding of the material.

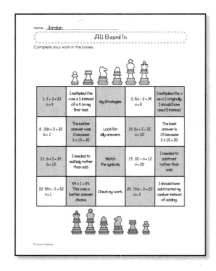

CD-104533 ■ © Carson-Dellosa

All Boxed In

Complete your work in the boxes.

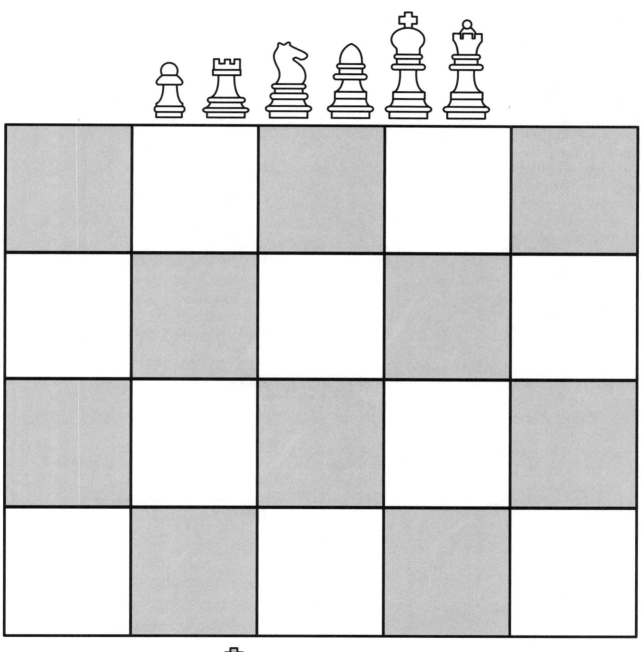

© Carson-Dellosa

Taking Time to Reflect

Subject Area Uses
- All subject areas

Skills
- Self-reflecting
- Organizing and analyzing

Purpose
Students have the opportunity to increase learning when opportunities are available for them to reflect on their learning. Taking Time to Reflect is designed to allow students to think about recently completed tasks and the steps they took to complete them. The organizer also encourages students to think about their own strengths and weaknesses so that they may set new and future goals. The organizer is useful in all subject areas and with students of all ability levels.

Using This Graphic Organizer
Have students answer each question on Taking Time to Reflect after completing a task. Then, have students list what they were trying to accomplish and follow the clock as they analyze their processes and the outcomes of their goals. Ask students to reflect on and list what they have learned and what they think they could do differently.

The organizer is useful in many other ways:

- Self-reflecting on a behavior in class and taking ownership of the action and discussing the process to change the behavior
- Organizing and analyzing information about skills needed to complete a math task; seeing the success from hard work
- Reflecting on an assessment, a research project, or a group task
- Reflecting on standardized testing
- Reviewing work from a science experiment where the hypothesis was incorrect

Primary Model

This first-grade student used Taking Time to Reflect to look back on her work while completing a writing assignment. Because this was the first time the class had used workstations, the organizer helped the student understand that she needed to follow basic classroom procedures and workstation directions to accomplish her task. The organizer also provided feedback for the teacher and allowed him to determine what he would change if the class used workstations again.

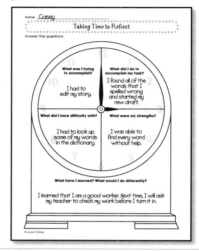

Intermediate Model

This fifth-grade student used Taking the Time to Reflect for a homework assignment to reflect on his science project. The teacher asked the students to complete a self-assessment. By using the organizer, the student was able to see his own strengths and weaknesses.

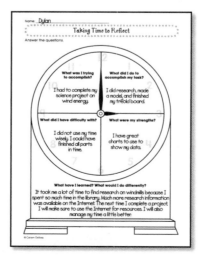

CD-104533 ■ © Carson-Dellosa

Name: _____

Taking Time to Reflect

Answer the questions.

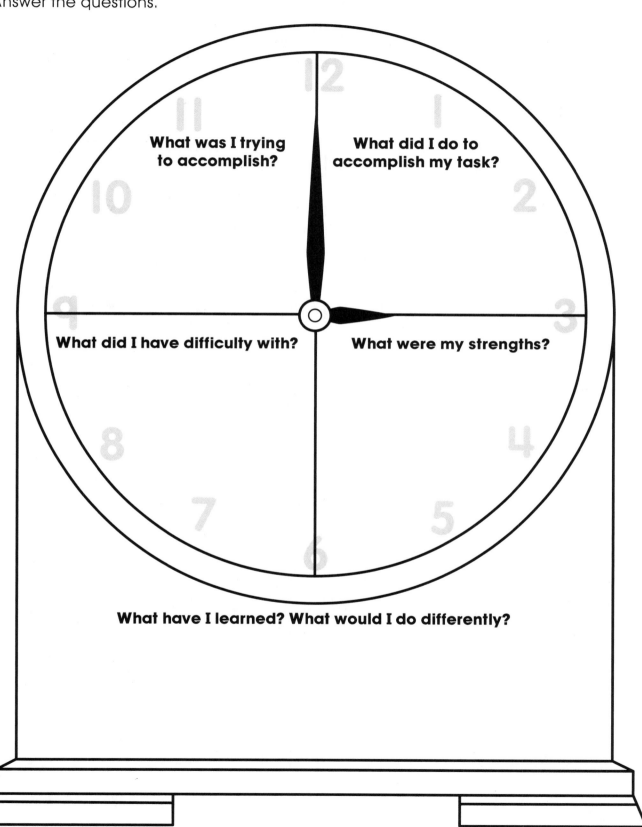

What was I trying
to accomplish?

What did I do to
accomplish my task?

What did I have difficulty with?

What were my strengths?

What have I learned? What would I do differently?

© Carson-Dellosa

Subject Area Uses

- All subject areas

Skills

- Goal setting
- Formulating and constructing plans
- Assessing and evaluating goals

Purpose

Goal setting is an important life skill for any student. Inching Our Way to Success enables students to document the steps needed to set and meet goals and stay organized along the way. The organizer also helps students visualize their paths while taking the steps toward meeting their goals. The organizer is useful in all subject areas and with students of all ability levels.

Using This Graphic Organizer

Model the use of Inching Our Way to Success with a whole group, a small group, or an individual student. Once the students have identified the goals or the topics of study, model how to move from one circle to the next to set goals.

The organizer is useful in many other ways:

- Setting goals in a primary classroom for a student having difficulty following directions
- Setting academic goals for a student who is not passing a subject
- Creating a plan for a student who needs to read a larger variety of genres
- Developing a plan to prepare for standardized testing
- Creating long-term and short-term goals

Primary Model

This first-grade student used Inching Our Way to Success to reflect on and set goals on a particular behavior he was exhibiting in class. By using the organizer, the student was able to determine the steps he should take to improve and what rewards he might earn if he met his goal.

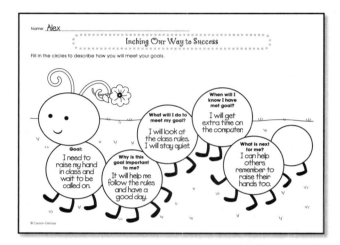

Intermediate Model

This fourth-grade student used Inching Our Way to Success to set goals to improve his grades. By using the organizer, the student was able to assess his grades and realize what steps he could take to improve them.

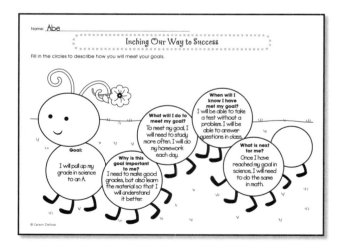

CD-104533 © Carson-Dellosa

Name: _____

Inching Our Way to Success

Fill in the circles to describe how you will meet your goals.

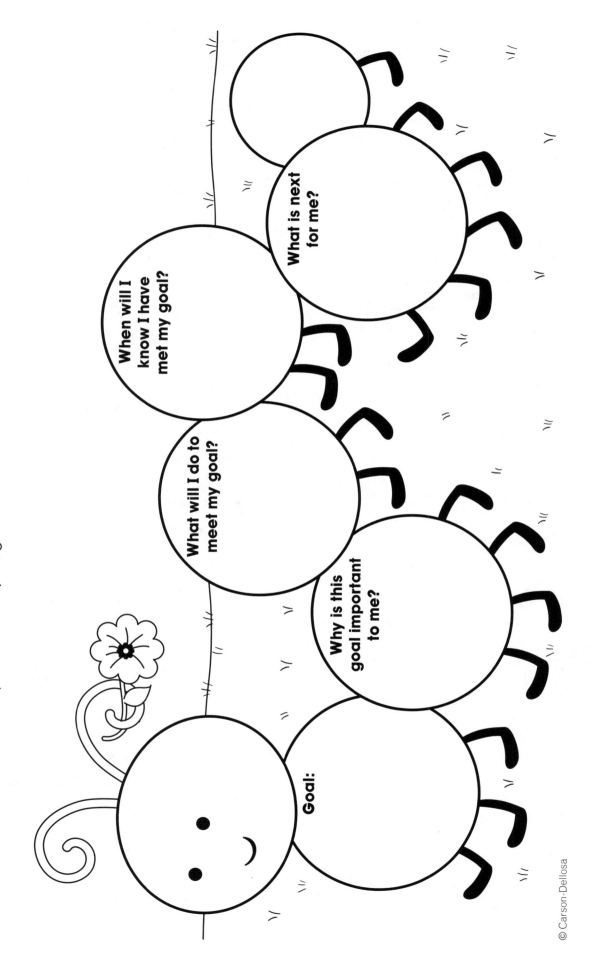

When will I know I have met my goal?

What is next for me?

What will I do to meet my goal?

Why is this goal important to me?

Goal:

© Carson-Dellosa

Subject Area Uses
- All subject areas

Skills
- Writing student contracts
- Goal setting

Purpose
Learning or behavioral contracts are agreements between teachers and students and may include parents or guardians as well. These contracts may identify what students need to learn or do and how they will learn or do it, as well as how and when the students will be evaluated. The Actions Speak Louder Than Words contract helps students make deliberate decisions and allows them to have more input in their learning. By using the organizer, students have support during those times when they are struggling academically or behaviorally or when they simply need help with organizing tasks.

Using This Graphic Organizer
Model the use of Actions Speak Louder Than Words in a small group or individual setting. Explain the contract to students and help them set goals while working through each step.

The organizer is useful in many other ways:

- Mapping out independent reading goals
- Creating an agreement to improve behavior
- Setting goals to improve test scores

Primary Model

This first-grade student used Actions Speak Louder Than Words with his teacher to help him set behavioral goals for the week. By using the organizer, the student was able to discuss the types of behaviors he needed to improve and have input into the types of things that might motivate him to meet his goals.

Intermediate Model

This fourth-grade student used Actions Speak Louder Than Words to set academic goals for the first nine weeks of school. The student, her parent, and her teacher were able to meet and collaboratively discuss what improvements the student needed to make, as well as how and when the goals would be evaluated. By using the organizer, the student was able to understand what steps she would need to take for improvement and also what consequences might arise if she did not work hard to meet her goals.

 CD-104533 © Carson-Dellosa

Name: _____

Actions Speak Louder Than Words

Complete and sign the contract.

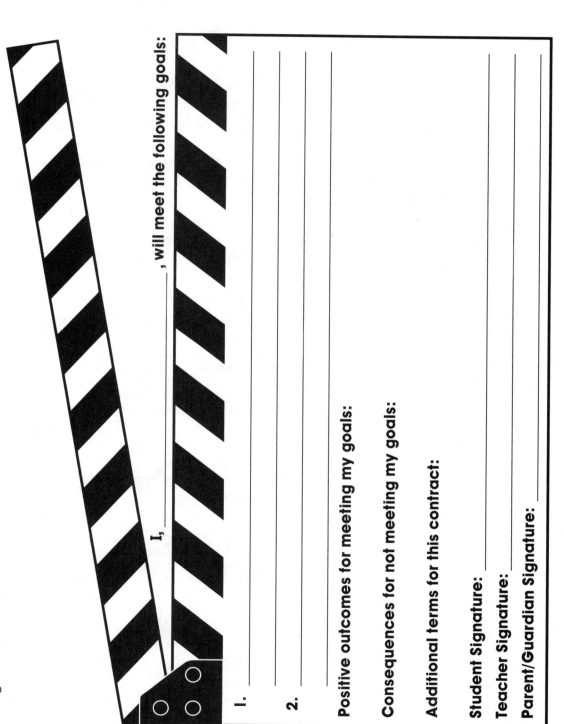

I, _____, will meet the following goals:

1. _____

2. _____

Positive outcomes for meeting my goals: _____

Consequences for not meeting my goals: _____

Additional terms for this contract: _____

Student Signature: _____

Teacher Signature: _____

Parent/Guardian Signature: _____

© Carson-Dellosa

Assignment Banners

Subject Area Uses
- All subject areas

Skills
- Planning and organizing
- Setting goals

Purpose
Students who are well organized are able to be more independent and rely less on their teachers or parents to keep up with daily assignments. Assignment Banners is an organizer that allows students to plan and organize their schedules, whether academic or outside of school. Learning to be organized is a great skill for students to learn and will benefit them throughout their professional and personal lives.

Using This Graphic Organizer
Assignment Banners provides a unique way to help students stay organized for homework or to practice scheduling needs throughout the week at school or home. Have students use the hanging banners to record their information each day. For example, if a student has a spelling test on Friday, he would list that, as well as place reminders on the other days to study the spelling words.

The organizer is useful in many other ways:

- Planning and scheduling school assignments, chores, or other responsibilities
- Organizing spelling words or other subject area topics to practice over the course of a week rather than waiting until the night before the test
- Emphasizing good work as a reward chart
- Creating a test or quiz schedule for the week to keep track of testing

Primary Model

This kindergarten student used Assignment Banners as a tool to plan for a spelling test on the upcoming Friday. The student studied two words each day to practice learning the -at rhyme. On Friday, the student was able to create words of her own using that rhyme.

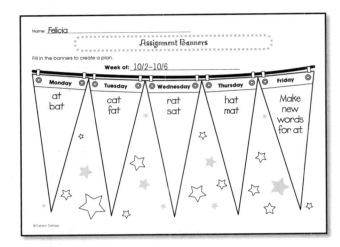

Intermediate Model

This fourth-grade student used the Assignment Banners organizer as a homework chart. The chart enabled the student to plan around extracurricular activities and prepare for formal assessments.

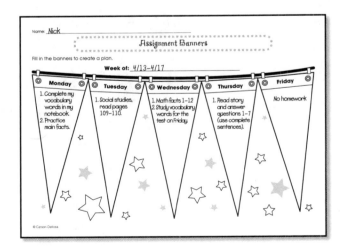

 © Carson-Dellosa

Name: _____

Assignment Banners

Fill in the banners to create a plan.

Week of: _____

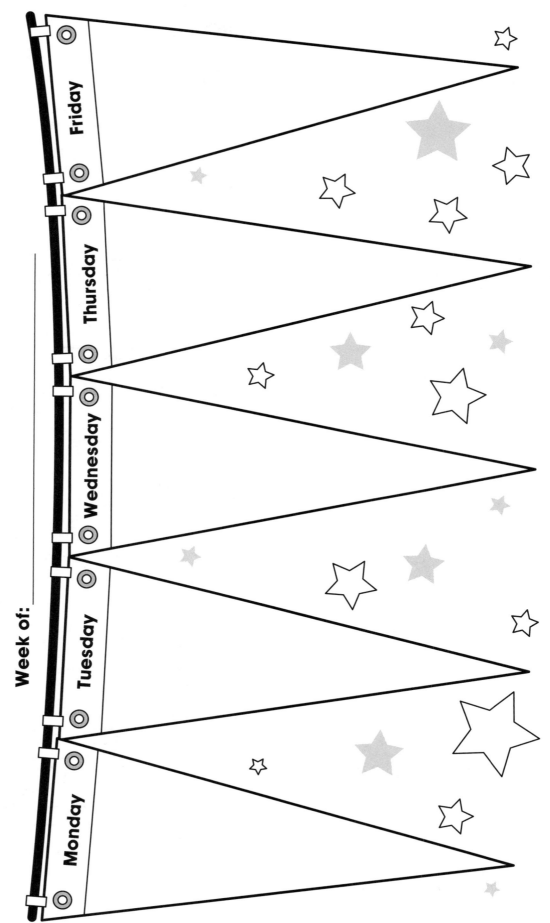

© Carson-Dellosa

Reading Log

Subject Area Uses
- Reading (all genres)

Skills
- Record keeping
- Classifying
- Analyzing and assessing

Purpose
The Reading Log allows students to systematically record the books that they have read and to keep track of their reading success. As students develop into independent readers, it is very important for them to have a purpose to their reading. The Reading Log organizer provides students with a visually engaging record to keep track of their work.

Using This Graphic Organizer
As students begin to mature as readers, it is very important for them to be able to track and analyze their reading levels, types of books, and comprehension abilities, as well as to see that their reading has a purpose. Have students record information in the Reading Log, including the date, the title, and the pages read. Also have students use the record of genres located in the body of each beaver to determine what types of books they are reading.

The organizer is useful in many other ways:

- Social Studies: keeping track of articles or informational text
- Language Arts: recording reading of a variety of genres
- At Home: recording reading at home

Primary Model

This second-grade teacher used the Reading Log organizer to assess a student's at-home reading. The organizer enabled the teacher to see that the student was ready to progress to chapter books so that he might have more of a challenge.

Name: Lane

Reading Log

Record your reading in the organizer.

Date	Title	Pages Read	Genre	Initials
10/1	And You Can Come Too	1–End	6	LS
10/3	Ants	1–End	6	LS
10/4	Apples and How They Grow	1–9	6	LS
10/5	↓	10–20	6	LS
10/6	Who Was Helen Keller?	1–19	8	LS
10/7	↓	20–32	8	LS
10/15	Who Was Abraham Lincoln?	1–End	8	LS

Fiction:
1. Realistic
2. Fantasy
3. Historical
4. Mystery
5. Fairy/Folk Tales

Nonfiction:
6. Informational
7. How-To
8. Biography
9. Autobiography
10. Sports

Other:
11. Poetry
12. Magazine
13. Catalog
14. Comic

© Carson-Dellosa

Intermediate Model

This fifth-grade student used the Reading Log to record her reading in the reading center. The organizer became a tool that the teacher and the student used during conferencing. The student realized that by choosing other genres, she would have more variety in her reading.

Name: Quinn

Reading Log

Record your reading in the organizer.

Date	Title	Pages Read	Genre	Initials
1/6	Abe Lincoln Remembers	1–14	8	QR
1/7	↓	15–End	8	QR
1/12	Fine Lines	1–End	3	QR
1/14	Five Brave Explorers	1–End	1	QR
1/19	Shoeshine Girl	1–23	1	QR
1/25	Georgia's Bones	1–20	2	QR
1/26	↓	21–46	2	QR

Fiction:
1. Realistic
2. Fantasy
3. Historical
4. Mystery
5. Fairy/Folk Tales

Nonfiction:
6. Informational
7. How-To
8. Biography
9. Autobiography
10. Sports

Other:
11. Poetry
12. Magazine
13. Catalog
14. Comic

© Carson-Dellosa

CD-104533 ■ © Carson-Dellosa

Name: _____

Reading Log

Record your reading in the organizer.

Date	Title	Pages Read	Genre	Initials

Fiction:
1. Realistic
2. Fantasy
3. Historical
4. Mystery
5. Fairy/Folk Tales

Nonfiction:
6. Informational
7. How-To
8. Biography
9. Autobiography
10. Sports

Other:
11. Poetry
12. Magazine
13. Catalog
14. Comic

© Carson-Dellosa

A Packed Portfolio

Subject Area Uses
- All subject areas

Skills
- Collecting and organizing information
- Analyzing collections of materials
- Reflecting on work completed

Purpose
In any subject area, portfolios are useful instructional strategies to help students self-reflect and understand their academic work. A portfolio functions as an illustration to show students, teachers, and parents a range of goals, levels, and completed assignments. A Packed Portfolio is an engaging organizer that does just that. By building the student portfolio of specific pieces, the organizer enables students to explain the reasons for their choices so that they may better analyze future work.

Using This Graphic Organizer
Model the use of A Packed Portfolio by placing a large copy on the board and showing students how to list specific entries, their dates, and explanations of what they are on the organizer.

The organizer is useful in many other ways:

- Documenting a collection of student writing
- Serving as a table of contents for a collection of best work across subject areas
- Recording work that students are most proud of

Primary Model
This first-grade student used A Packed Portfolio to prepare for an open house where she would show her best work to her family. The organizer, which served as a table of contents, gave the student, her family, and her teacher insight into the type of work the student was doing during the first month of school. It also highlighted the student's strengths.

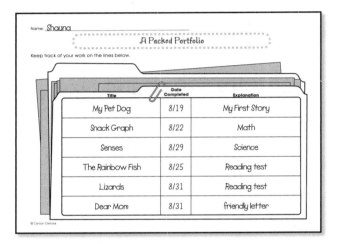

Intermediate Model
This fifth-grade student used A Packed Portfolio to showcase his writing assignments over the course of the year. The organizer served as a summary of the type of writing the student completed and also became a record of assessment for both the student and the teacher.

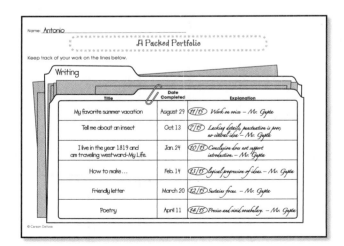

 © Carson-Dellosa

Name: _____

A Packed Portfolio

Keep track of your work on the lines below.

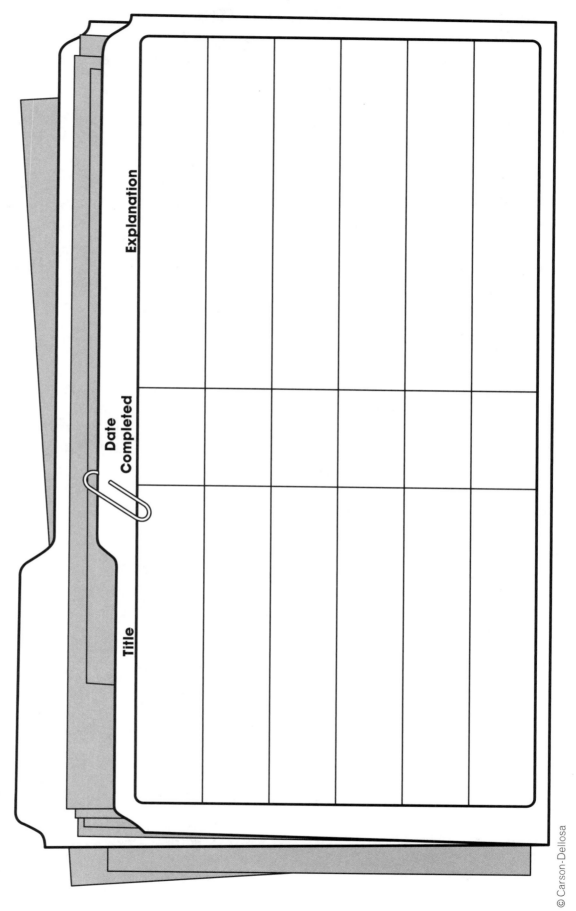

Title	Date Completed	Explanation

© Carson-Dellosa

Resources

Cunningham, P., Allingon, R. *Classrooms That Work: They Can All Read and Write* (Allyn & Bacon, 2010)

Darch, C., Carnine, D. and Kameenui, E. "The role of graphic organizers and social structure in content area instruction" (*Journal of Reading Behavior*, 1986)

Horton, S. V., Lovitt, T. C. and Bergerud, D. "The effectiveness of graphic organizers for three classifications of secondary students in content area classes" (*Journal of Learning Disabilities*, 1990)

Lane, B. *After the End: Teaching and Learning Creative Revision.* (Heinemann, 1992)

Marzano, R., Pickering, D. and Pollock, J. *Classroom Instruction That Works: Research-Based Strategies for Increasing Student Achievement* (Prentice Hall, 2004)

Meyen, E., Vergason, G. and Whelan, R. *Strategies for Teaching Exceptional Children in Inclusive Settings* (Love Publishing, 1996)

Tomlinson, C. A. *The Differentiated Classroom: Responding to the Needs of All Learners* (Prentice Hall, 1999)

CD-104533 ■ © Carson-Dellosa